TIBETAN
SACRED DANCE

TIBETAN
SACRED DANCE

A JOURNEY INTO THE RELIGIOUS AND FOLK TRADITIONS

ELLEN PEARLMAN

Inner Traditions
Rochester, Vermont

Inner Traditions
One Park Street
Rochester, Vermont 05767
www.InnerTraditions.com

Library of Congress Cataloging-in-Publication Data
Pearlman, Ellen.
  Tibetan sacred dance : a journey into the religious and folk
traditions / Ellen Pearlman.
       p. cm.
Includes bibliographical references and index.
  ISBN 0-89281-918-9
  1. Buddhism—China—Tibet—Rituals. 2. Cham (Dance) 3. Achi lhamo
(Dance) 4. Dance—Religious aspects—Buddhism. 5. Tibet
(China)—Social life and customs. I. Title.
  BQ7695 .P43 2002
  294.3'437—dc21   2002013105

Printed and bound in Hong Kong

10 9 8 7 6 5 4 3 2 1

Text design by Virginia Scott Bowman, layout by Cynthia Ryan Coad
This book was typeset in Garamond and Stone Sans with Village-Roman Titling and Contemporary MT1 as display typefaces.

Illustration Credits

Cover photographs: (upper left) sacred dance in Bhutan, copyright 1968 by Chögyam Trungpa, courtesy of Diana J. Mukpo and the Shambhala Archives; all other images by Ellen Pearlman—(upper right) the old man Tashi Chopa; (lower left) ging, beating a drum; (lower right) young monks at Rumtek Monastery, Sikkim.

Chapter title ornament: Knot of Eternity, Rumtek Monastery, Sikkim.

Decorative ornaments (see pages v and 9) and background (see page viii) used throughout book: From the saddle gear of the Fifth Karmapa, 10th century, Sikkim.

Pages 6, 65, 66, and 169: Sacred dance in Bhutan by Chögyam Trungpa. Copyright 1968 by Chögyam Trungpa. From the collection of the Shambhala Archives. Used by permission of Diana J. Mukpo and the Shambhala Archives.

Page 15 (top): Courtesy of the Shelley & Donald Rubin Collection. http://himalayanart.org.

Page 15 (bottom): Courtesy of the collection of Peter the Great, Museum of Anthropology and Ethnology of the World, St. Petersburg, Russia. Photographs copyright Ellen Pearlman.

Pages 16 (top) and 70 (left): Courtesy of the Museum für Indische Kunst, Berlin.

Pages 20 and 31: Courtesy of the Wise Albums, collection of Sir Ouseley (1770–1884), the British Library.

Pages 25, 62, 99, 119, 120, 150, 164, and 167: Courtesy of the European manuscript collection of the British Library. Photographs by Sir Charles Bell and others.

Page 29: *Vision of Yeshe Tsogyal* by Chögyam Trungpa. Used by permission of Diana J. Mukpo.

Page 60: Copyright International Museum for Tibetan Traditions, collection of Nari Ronge.

Page 67: Courtesy of the British Museum.

Pages 103 and 142: Courtesy of the Performing Arts Library of the New York City Public Library.

Pages 108, 114, 127 (top right), 129, 130, 131, 133, 145, 147, and 163: Courtesy of the Tibetan Institute of Performing Arts. Photos by Kim Yeshe.

Pages 127 (bottom) and 128: Copyright Anna Fuentes/GlobalPhoto.

This book is dedicated to Chögyam Trungpa Rinpoche,
His Holiness the Fourteenth Dalai Lama,
and Khempo Tsultrim Gyamtso, who taught me the dharma

ACKNOWLEDGMENTS

First and foremost, I would like to thank Valrae Reynolds, Curator of the Tibetan Collection at the Newark Museum, who offered her unwavering and unstinting support for my writing this book in the first place. So many other people helped throughout this process, especially my editors, Jeanie Levitan and Nancy Yeilding, publisher Ehud Sperling, editorial assistant Jess Matthews, and the entire wonderful staff of Inner Traditions. Others to thank are His Holiness the Fourteenth Dalai Lama; the Sixteenth Karmapa; the Sakya Trizan; Lobsang Samten and the monks of Namgyal Monastery; Tibetan Institute of Performing Arts; Chaksampa; the monks of Ganden Shartse; Drepung Losaling; the Sakya monks; Lopon Tenzin Namdak of the Bön lineage; the Gyuto monks; Lama Tenzin Samdev of the Kalachakra Temple in St. Petersburg, Russia; Rinchen Dharlo of The Tibet Foundation; Lhakdor at the Office of Tibet in Dharamsala, India; Jennifer Howe and the ever helpful librarians at the British Library; the late Dr. Michael Aris for recommending the Wise Albums Collection; Nari Ronge for sharing the magnificent Tibetan slide library in Bonn, Germany; Marc Bennett for the photograph; Cecilia Yu and Nils Nielson and Lize Maria Sneep for London and Amsterdam accommodations; Dr. Miranda Shaw and Dr. Georges Dreyfus for discussions through the years; Cinna Hunter, for reading an early version of the manuscript; Paula Litzky, for her advice; the staff of Dechen Choling in France for allowing me to use the yellow room to complete this manuscript; the staff at Samadhi Cushions in Vermont for its help; Roxanne Gupta for her generosity; and Amy Ritchie for putting up with my schedule.

CONTENTS

PROLOGUE

When I first journeyed to Dharamsala, India, home of the Dalai Lama in exile, I had been practicing Buddhism for only a few years. Following the traditional first step on the path—taking refuge in the Buddha, *dharma* (teachings), and *sangha* (community of practitioners)—I went and took refuge under a Tibetan lama, Kalu Rinpoche, in Cambridge, Massachusetts, in 1974.

His Holiness the 14th Dalai Lama underneath the Bodhi Tree, Bodh Gaya, India, 1977

Opposite: Dorje Trollo, Namgyal Monastery, Dharamsala, India

Inspired to get closer to the source of Tibetan Buddhism, in 1977 I traveled to Dharamsala, where the exotic Tibetan culture-in-exile transplanted to India both baffled and magnetized me. I had no idea just how lucky I was to meander unimpeded around Namgyal Monastery, the monastic compound of His Holiness, the Dalai Lama watching in awe as monks in rough crimson robes—studying for their degree of Geshe, or Ph.D. in philosophy—smacked their *malas* (rosaries) together as they made a particularly invigorating point in their logic debates.

One overcast and soft gray afternoon I noticed Tibetans hanging around the complex speaking excitedly. Out of the corner of my eye I saw a group of dancers *whoosh* by in colorful and ornamented brocade costumes. Fortunately, I happened to be carrying a crude box camera and instinctively reached for it, clicking as they rushed by on their way to perform a sacred ceremony. Intrigued, I followed. Although I wasn't allowed to enter the shrine room, I was able to watch through the open door.

MUSICIANS
FOLLOWING
CHAM DANCERS,
DHARAMSALA,
1977

PREPARING CHAM
COSTUMES,
DHARAMSALA,
1977

Monks pursed their lips and blew through enormous long horns, followed by blasts from other monks playing shorter trumpets. The hair on my arms stood on end and I felt something no music had ever stirred in me before, a sense of coming back into myself. Dancing slowly and deliberately, in measured synchronized steps, the dancers turned while the cymbals clashed and a bass drum beat out a slow, continuous rhythm.

I don't remember how long this went on but I do remember that my mind, literally, stopped. All concepts drained away and I could focus only on the spectacle in front of me. I didn't know then that I was experiencing *bodhicitta,* a basic unobscured state of clarity and emptiness. I didn't understand what I was seeing, nor did I know what it meant. I was clueless about what the monks were practicing—a special kind of meditation that used body, speech, and mind. I just knew I felt at peace, and returned to an inner tranquillity I knew was there but didn't know how to find.

The profound impact of my first encounter with Tibetan sacred dance led me to undertake a long search to understand what I had seen and experienced. That journey led me deep into Tibetan culture, history, and spiritual practices, and into the story of one religion, Buddhism, taking precedence over another, the ancient, shamanistic Bön religion that existed when Buddhism was first introduced into Tibet. I've had wonderful teachers, friends, and guides along the way to explain the legends and symbols, the meanings and functions, of both kinds of Tibetan dance—the *Cham,* or "lama," dance performed by monks and *Achi Lhamo,* or folk dance. I learned that Cham (Tibetan for "a dance") serves a ritualized, sacred purpose, while Achi Lhamo (Tibetan for "sister goddess") is performed for entertainment, to retell historical legends, and for general merriment.

I invite you to share my journey through the wonders and mysteries of Tibetan dance in the pages that follow.

1 CHAM:
Sacred Monastic Dance

In a meditative state . . . the dance comes out of that . . .
In tantra oneself becomes the Buddha.

—Lobsang Samten, ritual dance master of
the Namgyal monks

Only in meditation are the methods of chanting
and instrumental playing revealed.

—His Holiness, the Sixteenth Gylwya Karmapa

CHAM DANCE CIRCLE,
BHUTAN, 1968. PHOTO BY
CHÖGYAM TRUNGPA

Each year—on the twenty-ninth day of the twefth month of the Tibetan calendar—at Namgyal College in Dharamsala, a small procession of ritual masters, horn blowers, cymbal players, drummers, and a master of ceremonies walk under a canopy through the courtyard. The trumpet player blows a silver-and-jewel-encrusted human thighbone. Monks follow them carrying wands of incense and sprinkle blessed water in a vase with a peacock feather sprouting from its crown. Then dancers wearing heavy black hats and carrying swords and shields enter the shrine to perform the Black Hat dance, one of the most important and beautiful dances done by Tibetan Buddhist monks.

The Black Hat dance refers to an incident in Tibetan history dating from the ninth century. In 838 C.E. Lang Darma, a practitioner of the ancient Bön religion, ascended to the throne by killing his brother. Once in power he initiated full-scale persecutions of Buddhist monasteries, forcing Buddhist monks to disrobe, and desecrated scores of temples. In 842 C.E. a monk called Lhalungpa Pelgyi Dorje mysteriously appeared in Lhasa, the capital, wearing a black robe and a big black hat. He began dancing outside of Lang Darma's residence and was asked to enter and perform his dance for the king, which he did. At the climax of the presentation he drew a small bow and arrow out from underneath the long, flowing sleeves of his robe and shot Lang Darma right in the eye, killing him. During the ensuing confusion, Pelgyi Dorje fled the scene on a horse covered with black soot. As they waded through a river, the soot washed off the horse, turning it back to its original color, a brilliant white. At the same time, Pelgyi Dorje turned his black robe inside out, displaying its white inner lining.

RADONG, SACRED LONG HORNS, IN OPENING CEREMONY

MONKS BLOWING
THIGHBONE AND
OTHER HORNS

OPPOSITE: BLACK
HAT DANCER
WEARING SAKYA-STYLE
RITUAL HAT

None of the search party was looking for a white-robed man on a white horse, so Pelgyi Dorje escaped to the eastern district of Kham, where he joined the group of persecuted monks and translators still carrying on the Buddhist tradition. Once there, he returned to his meditative life. His seemingly murderous deed displays *bodhisattva* action—action performed for the benefit of all beings. It illustrates the concept of killing another human being for the sake of others, in order to dispel greater evil and save thousands of lives.

As this story shows, the Black Hat dance—like all Tibetan dance—is both an essential part of the rich history of Tibet and inextricably woven into Tibet's own unique brand of Buddhism. It is fortunate that a nation's culture could be presented so clearly through dance. What is even more astonishing is the active and instrumental role played by dance in the unfolding of key historic events.

BLACK HAT DANCERS,
NEW YORK CITY, 1991

ENTERING THE WORLD OF CHAM

The story of Tibetan dance directly parallels the story of the growth of Buddhism inside Tibet. Unfortunately, little of this intertwined history was documented, and until quite recently almost nothing on this fascinating subject was available in the English language. Most of the traditions of Tibetan dance in both its forms—the mesmerizing sacred tradition and the theatrical folk

CAVE PAINTING
SHOWING ANCIENT
ORIGINS OF DANCE
IN CENTRAL ASIA

ANCIENT
MONGOLIAN
SHAMAN WITH
DRUM

version—were passed down through initiations, secret teachings, and special schools. Because of the oral nature of this transmission, it is difficult to know exactly what is legend and what is real in a saga filled with outrageous teachers, court intrigue, visions, secret practices, and supernatural powers. But the backdrop for this saga is the very real interaction between two religions, Buddhism and Bön.

From the time of its first introduction in Tibet, around 173 B.C.E., Buddhism spent centuries vying with the Bön religion for influence and favor in the courts of Tibet's rulers. Bön—believed to have originated in the ancient land of Tazig (referring generally to the direction of Persia)—was imbued with north Asian shamanism and practices of magic, with roots going back to the early Paleolithic period. Bön later established itself in Zhang Zhung, a kingdom in the central Asian part of Iran near Mount Kailash. It is said that during the fifth century B.C.E. a mass migration of Iranians came to northern Tibet, bringing Bön with them. Many of these Iranians mixed with Tibetans, and the Bön religion flourished.

As with any animistic form of worship, the Bön followers (known as Bönpo) believed that all the elements of the natural world—rocks, trees, animals, sky, earth, underworld, lakes—were possessed by spirits. In this worldview, a shamanlike human figure would often become the intermediary between the spirit and human worlds. Special initiations and training enabled the shamans to understand how energy manifests in both the body and the outside environment. They would internally consecrate and purify their minds to become more externally sensitive, allowing them to mediate between symbolic languages displayed through performance, music, and dance. The shaman would "die" and "dismember" himself in a dream world, then come back vibrantly healed from his ordeal to share his fresh insights with others in his tribe. These insights were profound and often prophetic and helped the people survive the coming seasons.

The two main Bön gods were Cha, the god of chance, and Yang, the god of fortune. These deities were pacified through blood sacrifice, dance, and song. Ancient followers of the Bön religion believed that they had to eat and digest their object of worship in order to become one with it (a belief not shared by the two modern Bön schools, which disown such practices). Each fall the priests performed a mass sacrifice of one thousand wild asses. In the springtime the legs of a hind, a female red deer, were exchanged as ransom for new life. In the frigid winter, a blood sacrifice was made to assuage the Bön god called Bön-lha and in the summer there was yet another killing to offer to the original Bön master Shenrab.[1] Bön practices also included dance for religious and royal rituals: "The Bön performed dances during the New Year in order to obtain the (blessings) of the Mnga' Thang, the supernatural forces present in the person of the ruler, and maintain the cosmic and social order intact with the working order."[2]

Although Buddhism grew in influence over the centuries after its introduction, Bön prevailed as the court religion at the time when Tibet's history begins in a more established form, with the rule of King Songtsen Gampo, who reigned 627–49 C.E. His father—King Namri Songtsen of the Yarlung Valley, an area southeast of Lhasa considered to be the cradle of Tibetan civilization—had started unifying the various warring, seminomadic tribes in the valley, but had been assassinated when Songtsen Gampo was thirteen.

TONPA SHENRAB, FOUNDER OF BÖN

SONGTSEN GAMPO, ONE OF THE THREE GREAT KINGS

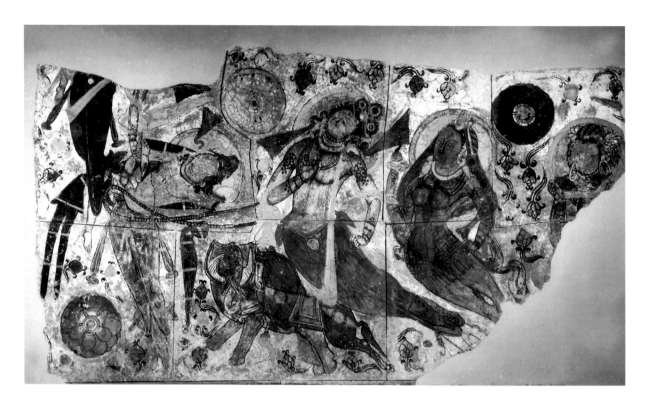

Songtsen Gampo continued his father's legacy of uniting the tribal factions and went on to conquer more of the surrounding territories. He eventually moved his capital to Lhasa, where he began building a fortress on Marpori (Red Mountain), which was later developed into the renowned Potala Palace.

Songtsen Gampo cemented his alliances with the provinces by marrying three women from various regions of Tibet, a practice common at that time. He then made two more marriages of alliance, the first with the Nepalese princess Bhrikuti (also known as Besa or Tritsun) in 632 C.E., and the second nine years later with the daughter of the Chinese emperor, Princess Wen Cheng Kongjo. They each arrived with magnificent dowries, including the Jowo Shakyamuni Buddha brought by Princess Wen Cheng, now the most sacred image in Tibet. Both women were devout Buddhists and they strongly influenced the king to adopt Buddhism, fostering its first important inroad into the royal court. Over the objections of influential Bön courtiers, Songtsen Gampo formally embraced Buddhism as Tibet's state religion. Eventually Princess Bhrikuti became symbolized by the legendary goddess Green Tara, an embodiment of compassion, while Princess Wen Cheng symbolically came to be known as the lovely goddess White Tara. The king also promoted the establishment of a written Tibetan script and grammar so that the Indian Buddhist texts written in Sanskrit could be transcribed into a new, unique Tibetan alphabet.

Some hundred years later, King Trisong Deutsen (742–800 C.E.) came on the scene. Considered one of Tibet's three greatest kings, he ruled Tibet during a time when it was perpetually at war, expanding the territories that the four kings since Songtsen Gampo had managed to secure, ranging from modern Pakistan to northwest India to northwest China.

Meanwhile, the powerful Bön ministers and clans had been opposing the adoption of Buddhism as the state religion ever since Songtsen's reign. The roots of the Bön religion were still strong among the people and they fiercely resisted a shift to Buddhism. King Trisong Deutsen embarked upon building temples and monasteries to spread Buddhist teachings and practices in Tibet. He invited Shantarakshita, a revered and learned Buddhist monk from India, to help secure Buddhism's place. But when several disasters struck—such as the Red Mountain Palace being struck by lightning, another palace being destroyed by a flood, and people and livestock being felled by disease— Shantarakshita understood that the local spirits, stirred up by Bön magic, were not happy and needed pacifying. He felt himself no match for the shamans, so he asked the king to invite the well-known Buddhist tantric adept Padmasambhava to defeat the magical excesses of the Bön shamans. A message was sent to Padmasambhava, who accepted the king's invitation. With his arrival in Tibet in 765 C.E., the stage was set for the first performance of Cham, the *Vajrakilaya* dance.

VAJRAKILAYA, THE DANCE OF THE THREE-SIDED RITUAL DAGGER

Also known as Guru Rinpoche, Padmasambhava was a master adept of the *Vajrayana*, the diamond thunderbolt, or tantric path of Buddhism. He came from Uddiyana (the modern Swat region of Afghanistan), an area famous during those times for producing master yogis. Padmasambhava means "lotus born." According to legend, the attendants of the local ruler's court in

King Trisong Deutsen, one of the three great kings

Opposite (top): The seven jewels of a worldly king: wheel, elephant, horse, minister, women, and jewel (general missing). Cave painting fragment from Dun-Huang, Museum für Indische Kunst, Berlin

Opposite (center): Potala Palace, winter seat of the Dalai Lama, pre-1958

Opposite (bottom): White Tara, dressed like a bodhisattva, with her right hand forming the *virada mudra* and her left hand forming the *vitarka mudra*

Uddiyana went out one day to cut fresh flowers for the palace and found an eight-year-old boy sitting on a lotus pad in the center of Lake Dhanakosha. King Indrabhuti, who had no sons, was overjoyed when informed of this wonder and decided to adopt the boy as his own child and heir.

Padmasambhava grew up in the palace and dutifully married a noble girl named Prabhadhari (also called Bhasadhara). As expected, he began to rule Uddiyana, his adopted father's kingdom. But royal life was not for him, just as it had not been for the Buddha, the Indian prince Siddhartha, and Padmasambhava abandoned the pleasures of the palace in order to practice tantric yoga. Eventually he became a *vidyadhara,* a master of tantric practices, skilled in the understanding of *terma* (hidden treasure) magic, rebirth, prolonging the life of others, neutralizing poison, having clear visions, walking on water, generating heat without clothes *(tumo),* and yogic running *(lung-gom-pa).* In one account his wrathful aspect was described as "he who subdues whatever needs to be subdued and whoever needs to be subdued and destroys whoever needs to be destroyed."

In order to help King Trisong Deutsen and Shantarakshita clear away all the Bön-invoked obstacles to their project of building Samye, the first Tibetan Buddhist monastery, Padmasambhava performed the powerful Vajrakilaya dance. According to the Fifth Dalai Lama, "The great religious master Padmasambhava performed this dance in order to prepare the ground for the Samye Monastery and to pacify the malice of the *lha* [local mountain god spirits] and *srin* [malevolent spirits] in order to create the most perfect conditions."[3] He went on to say that after Padmasambhava consecrated the ground, he erected a thread-cross—a web of colored thread woven around two sticks—to catch evil. Then the purifying energy of his dance forced the malevolent spirits into a skull mounted on top of a pyramid of dough. His tantric dance cleared away all the obstacles, enabling the monastery to be built in 767. The dance was memorialized by the construction of Vajrakilaya *stupas*—monuments honoring the ritual *kilya* (purba) daggers—at the cardinal points of the monastery, where they would prevent demonic forces from entering the sacred grounds.[4]

The protective power of Padmasambhava and the vajra kilya are reinvoked with each performance of the Vajrakilaya dance by Tibetan monks. Like all

OPPOSITE:
PADMASAMBHAVA,
KNOWN AS GURU
RINPOCHE. HIS
CONSORTS YESHE
TSOGYEL AND
MANDRABA ARE
ALSO DEPICTED.

18

TIBETAN SACRED DANCE

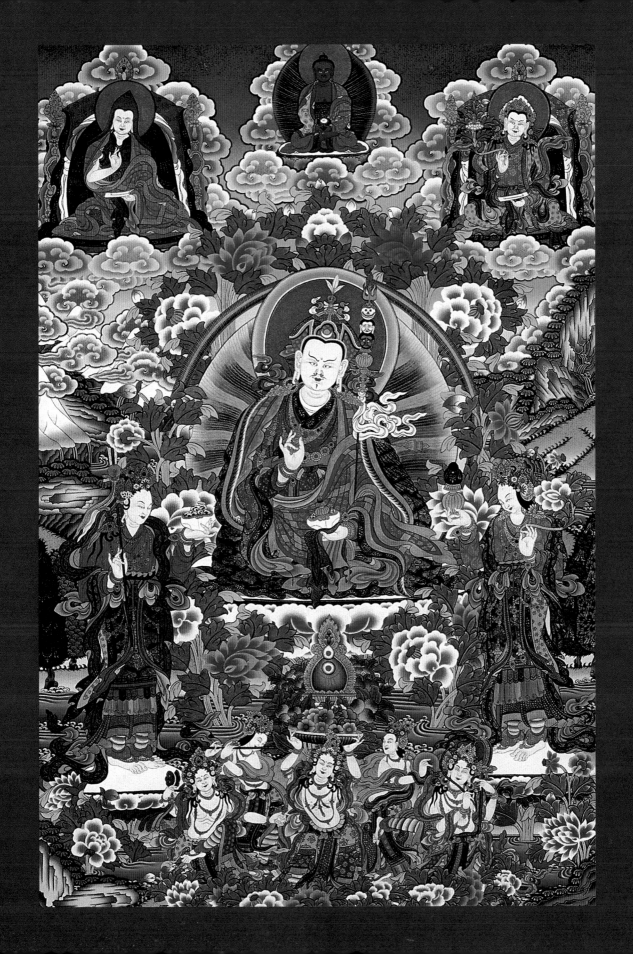

▣ Vajra Kilya ▣

These are notes from the painting in the Wise Collection at the British Library, which I first saw in 1990. The album states that in the 1860s an unidentified Buddhist lama from the western Himalayas in the 1860s met an Englishman, who commissioned the lama to produce a pictorial encyclopedia of the Tibetan physical and spiritual landscapes.

This color painting depicts the wrathful Padmasambhava, based on a sixteenth-century vision of the great master Pema Karpo. The lower part of the body is a three-pointed dagger *(purba)* that pierces the heart of one's own negativity. The blade emerges from the mouth of a sea serpent *(makara)*. In his right hand, Padmasambhava holds a vajra as a symbol of his power, while his left hand holds a scorpion, which he uses to annihilate spiritual materialism. Guru Rinpoche is surrounded by the Buddha Amitaba, the Bodhisattva Shadakshari (a four-armed form of Avalokiteshvara), the Bodhisattva Lokeshvara (a two-armed, red form of Avalokiteshvara), and a more peaceful manifestation of himself.

The lama in the upper left is Pema Karpo, who stands in a line of Tibetan mystics or *tertons* who discovered secret texts left behind by Padmasambhava and his consort Yeshe Tsoygel.

The two seated Kagyu lamas illustrate the close ties between the Nyingma and Kagyu sects.

Pema Karpo contributed twenty-four volumes of collected works on Tibetan Buddhist philosophy,

VAJRA KILYA OR "MAGIC DAGGER DEITY" OF THE WRATHFUL MANIFESTATION OF GURU RINPOCHE (PADMASAMBHAVA)

logic, literature, history, and astrology, which continue to be studied by all sects and traditions. He constructed the monastery of Druk Sangag Choling (the Dharma Garden of Secret Mantrayana) at Jar, in southern Tibet, and later transferred the seat of the Drukpa Order to this monastery.

Cham dances, it operates on two levels, the upper action, designed to achieve enlightenment, and the lower action, designed to destroy evil forces and obstacles. Impurity is transformed into purity through the dance, in which consciousness ritually enters as a demon and exits as a deity.

The dancers often hold a skull and scarf tied together and then attached to the hilt of a *purba,* another name for the Vajrakilaya ritual dagger. The scarf spreads the action quality of compassion, while the skull *(banda)* represents impermanence. The purba embodies qualities of body, speech, and mind, and its three blades symbolize passion, aggression, and ignorance. Symbolic offerings are made of the five substances of the human body—urine, excrement, semen, flesh, and blood. *Torma,* a roasted barley flour cake painted red, with sculpted butter ornaments, is offered, likely as a substitute for the animal sacrifices of earlier dance traditions, to get rid of negativities. The Vajrakilaya dance has seven stages, and was traditionally performed by combinations of either 13, 17, 21, or 23 monks, often each playing his own drum.

SAMYE MONASTERY, FIRST MONASTERY IN TIBET, FOUNDED BY PADMASAMBHAVA. PHOTO TAKEN BEFORE CULTURAL REVOLUTION

▣ The Dalai Lamas and Cham ▣

Gendun Drubpa—the lama who retroactively came to be considered the First Dalai Lama—foretold his own rebirth before his death in 1474, thus beginning the lineage of the Dalai Lamas. At death, the Dalai Lama is considered to go into a transitory realm called the *bardo,* where he remains for forty-nine days before being reborn as a child. Portentous signs are said to occur during this time of rebirth, including a surfeit of natural phenomena such as rainbows when no clouds are present. The child usually exhibits a healthy precociousness and certain physical characteristics such as special markings, webbing around the feet and hands, and a recognition of his predecessor's former possessions when they are shown to him by special monks who search for the next Dalai Lama.

The Third Dalai Lama, Sonam Gyatso (1543–88), then abbot of Drepung Monastery, was the first to be called by the honorific name of Dalai Lama, meaning "Ocean of Wisdom," a title given him by the Mongolian ruler Altan Khan after the Khan's conversion to Buddhism.

Of all the Dalai Lamas, the Fifth, Gyalwa Lobsang Gyatso (1618–82), had perhaps the most crucial influence on the survival of Tibetan sacred dance through his written treatise entitled *Chams Yig.* This beautiful work provides a minutely detailed explanation of all aspects of Tibetan dance. In 1645 the Fifth Dalai Lama, also known as the "Great Fifth," began construction of the Potala Palace on Red Mountain, where he moved in 1653, establishing it as the home of all the subsequent Dalai Lamas.

OPPOSITE: YOUNG MONKS TRAINING IN CHAM STEPS, RUMTEK MONASTERY, SIKKIM

THE FIFTH DALAI LAMA WITH *CHAMS YIG*

Another Dalai Lama known for his love of the dance was the Sixth, Gyalwa Tsangyang Gyatso (1683–1707), surely the least conventional of the Dalai Lamas. He had been found by the traditional methods of recognition, yet he absolutely refused to don his monastic robes at the age of twenty. He consorted openly with women, drank beer *(chang),* and let his hair grow down his back in long braids studded with semiprecious stones of turquoise and coral. He was famous and revered for his beautiful love poems to his many consorts. His biography mentions that he observed his dance master performing in the snow, a common technique of study at the time. He would watch the location of his master's footprints left in the snow and memorize the different "thunderbolt" steps. When he grew older, he chastised himself for watching these steps only for pure entertainment and not for spiritual growth, but later he did master them for deeply spiritual purposes.

Continued on page 24

A mystery persists to this day as to how the Sixth Dalai Lama died. Because he was so administratively lax and dissolute, a band of warring Mongolians was able to take control of Lhasa and arrest him in 1706. After two hundred monks from Drepung surrounded the Mongol camp where the Sixth was held and safely conducted him to the monastery, the leader of the Mongolian kidnappers became furious and threatened to attack. In order to spare Drepung, the Sixth agreed to go with the Mongols into exile. As they moved him toward the north, they let the Dalai Lama give blessings to the hordes of Tibetans who came to see him, alerted by word of mouth to his procession.

One evening, as the group camped near Lake Kokonor, the Dalai Lama emerged from his tent wearing a ritual dagger and the elaborate black hat and tantric garments of his predecessor, the Great Fifth. He said, "Whatever possessions are here with me, and especially this mystic dagger and this tantric costume, should be given to my reincarnation."[5] He then started playing his *damaru* drum as he performed a tantric dance. The wind whipped all around him and seemed to grow in intensity along with his dance. Some people even reported seeing sparks and fire in the whirlwind. As a grand finale, he leapt up and landed on the ground in a cross-legged meditation posture. People were speechless as the wind mysteriously died down. One of his attendants came up to him and burst into tears, believing that the Sixth Dalai Lama was dead, having practiced *powa*, the ejection of consciousness at the moment of death. Other stories relate that this was all a ruse, and that he managed to slip away to live out his life as a secluded practitioner.

TANTRIC DANCER PERFORMING A LEAPING STEP

THE THIRTEENTH DALAI LAMA, THUPTEN GYATSO, ON HIS THRONE IN THE JEWEL PARK PALACE WITHOUT HIS CEREMONIAL HAT

The Thirteenth Dalai Lama, Thupten Gyatso (1876–1933), is considered one of the greatest Dalai Lamas. Although strong in character, meditating four times a day and undertaking numerous retreats, he struggled to rule amid regional power struggles among British India, China, and Russia that culminated in the invasions of Tibet first by the British and later by the Chinese. A British mission headed by Colonel Francis Younghusband invaded Tibet in 1903–4, ostensibly to require Tibet to open up to trade. Although the British killed around a thousand Tibetans in order to reach Lhasa, an early travel journal describes a ceremonial send-off in which dance played a significant role:

"Before Colonel Younghusband's Mission left Lhasa, an open-air theatrical performance was given in their honor. It took place in the courtyard

OPEN-AIR THEATRICAL PERFORMANCE GIVEN IN HONOR OF THE DEPARTURE OF COLONEL YOUNGHUSBAND FROM LHASA. PAINTING BASED ON AN ORIGINAL PHOTOGRAPH

of the building in which the mission was quartered. The entertainment largely consisted of dancing, but there was also a play in which the principal parts were those of a demon and a boy. The dancing and acting were accompanied by the wildest gesticulations on the part of the actors."[6]

At the beginning of the British siege, the Thirteenth Dalai Lama fled Tibet for Mongolia. His exile in Mongolia profoundly affected him, causing such vivid dreams that he created a Cham based on them, the Old White Man from Mongolia dance. Before the Thirteenth died, he left behind instructions regarding his rebirth. He also left behind a prophecy, recorded eighteen years before the invasion of Tibet by China:

It may happen that here in the Center of Tibet the religious and secular administration may be attacked both from the outside and from the inside. Unless we can guard our own country, it will happen now that the Dalai and Panchen lamas, the Father and Son, the holders of the faith, the glorious rebirths, will be broken down and left without a name. As regards the monasteries and the priesthood, their lands and other properties will be destroyed. The administrative customs of the three religious Kings will be weakened, the officers of the state, ecclesiastical and secular, will find their lands seized and they themselves made to serve their enemies or wander about the country as beggars do. All beings will be sunk in great hardship and in overpowering fear. The days and nights will drag slowly into suffering.[7]

The current Dalai Lama, Tenzin Gyatso, was located by the official search party in Amdo province, near Kumbum Monastery. Born in 1935 to simple farming people, he proved to be an intelligent and serious child whose capacity for learning astonished even his tutors. He completed the most rigorous study for the Geshe degree in philosophy, a course taking over twelve years, when he was just twenty-three. Forced by the brutal invasion of the Communist Chinese to flee from Tibet into India in 1959, this Dalai Lama, the Fourteenth, has been confronted with a plethora of problems. He was immediately responsible for the welfare of the one hundred thousand Tibetans who went into exile with him. The Chinese program of desecration and destruction of monasteries, scriptures, and artworks, as well as the persecution and killing of

HIS HOLINESS THE FOURTEENTH DALAI LAMA PERFORMING THE *SADHANA* OF THE MANDALA OF THE MIND

learned monks in Tibet, has been so vicious that an entire millennium of cultural development is on the verge of being wiped out.

In 1960 the Dalai Lama moved to Dharamsala, in the foothills of the Himalayas, a site specifically selected for him by Prime Minister Nehru. Under his leadership, the government-in-exile began to rebuild itself, forming different departments like those of Home Affairs, Health, Security, Finance, Education, Religious and Cultural Affairs and Information, and International Relations. Education was a priority, as a generation of children in exile stood poised to lose their culture forever.

The Fourteenth Dalai Lama supported the founding of the Tibetan Institute of Performing Arts in 1959, the first such official organization created in exile, guided by a deep awareness that if these precious cultural forms are lost, there is no way to rekindle them. Now housed in Dharamsala, it trains young Tibetans in the arts of Achi Lhamo, costume and mask design, music, singing, drama, and theater. The monks of the Dalai Lama's own monastery, Namgyal, as well as those of several other monasteries, have begun to permanently reestablish ritual Cham dance.

CHAM AND THE DEVELOPMENT OF TIBETAN RELIGION

The Vajrakilaya dance represents one of the two main roads Tibetan Buddhism was to follow after the first performance of Cham by Padmasambhava and the establishment of the Samye Monastery. Since that time, the tantric or Vajrayana path of Tibetan Buddhism has been one of the most significant streams of Tibetan Buddhist wisdom, considered as a valid means for attaining enlightenment, revered for its ability to remove obstacles to the practice of dharma and to open the doors to limitless compassion.

Following the example of Padmasambhava, who had several female consorts, this path can involve the use of consorts for both men and women. During Padmasambhava's time, celibacy was not required of wandering yogis and yoginis. In fact, men and women often sought consorts who could help them with certain aspects of their spiritual practice. A female consort is called a *dakini,* which broadly means a female entity or emanation. *Dakini* literally translates as "sky dancer," and a dakini can be wrathful and horrific or peaceful and beautiful. Male consorts are referred to as *dakas* and can embody the same qualities.

Padmasambhava was the first and most important *terton,* a unique kind of tantric adept who conceals and reveals *terma,* secret teachings of the dharma. In tantric tradition women often carry the repository of the inner tantras, written down in a secret code language called Dakini Script. Padmasambhava's most famous consort was Yeshe Tsogyel, considered the most enlightened woman throughout Tibet. *Tsogyel* means "Dakini of the Ocean," supposedly because a lake increased in size when she was born. Padmasambhava transmitted all of

A WRATHFUL
DAKINI (TOP)
AND A PEACEFUL
DAKINI (BELOW)

*VISION OF YESHE
TSOGYAL.*
PAINTING BY
CHÖGYAM
TRUNGPA USED
BY PERMISSION OF
DIANA J. MUKPO

his secret oral teachings to her, and she helped him to hide those teachings both in physical form—in caves and under rocks, written on yellow parchment and sealed in gold and silver—and in the celestial form of visions and dreams. Terma continues to be rediscovered during times of spiritual crisis by tertons who are said to be incarnations of various aspects of Padmasambhava. Tertons must have the accompaniment of special female consorts in order to balance and harmonize their nervous system and subtle psychic channels. It is said that they can die if they do not obtain a consort or have the wrong consort.

The second path followed by Tibetan Buddhism from the time of Padmasambhava was that of a monastic tradition. First, seven Tibetan monks from noble families were ordained at Samye after being tested by Shantarakshita himself to make sure they were suited to the rigorous demands of monastic life. Later, three thousand men came from the thirteen principalities of Tibet[8] to apply to become monks, and three hundred of them succeeded. Padmasambhava picked 108 monks to begin the translation of sacred texts on a massive scale.

These two paths eventually evolved into four schools of Tibetan Buddhism—Nyingma, Sakya, Kagyu, and Gelug. The Nyingma or "Ancient Ones" school followed Padmasambhava, and were lay practitioners who were allowed to marry, while the later schools followed other teachers. The Sakya school, dating from the eleventh or twelfth century, honored teachers of the Sakya Gonpa, or "Gray Earth Mountain Monastery" (sakya means "Gray Earth"), built in southwestern Tibet in 1073. The Kagyu school of oral instruction developed an unbroken lineage of crazy wisdom teachings originating from the Indian Mahasiddha Tilopa (989–1069), to Naropa, to the great lay practitioner Marpa, and then on to the great ascetic yogi-poet Milarepa.

The Gelug school followed Tsongkhapa (1357–1419)—a great teacher from the Amdo province of eastern Tibet—who imposed a stricter asceticism on the Buddhist monastic community, built the three monasteries of Ganden, Sera, and Drepung, and wrote enormous commentaries on a wide array of topics. His *Lam Rim,* or "Stages on the Path," provides one of the most important bodies of written works in the Tibetan world. He was the teacher and uncle of the lama known retrospectively as the First Dalai Lama. He also established the great Monlam Prayer Festival—which features Cham and Achi Lhamo dances—held in Lhasa at the start of each new year.

have the same custom.

8. Represents Lopon Rinpoci, made of a colossal statue in wood. A man who moves the figure is concealed within the clothing. He has five wives.

9. A daughter of Zoar Raja named Lachum Metarana.

10. From the country of Gnat Ubchun. She has been thrown away by her parents. Lopun Rinpochi, who was performing penance there, saved her. Afterward he married her. Her mother's name was Pulbug and the girl's name was Puljung Kalasta.

11. Daughter of the Mon Raja named Zong Zong Gyalpo. Her name was Momo Tashi Kyenden. (*Note:* This is the princess Tashi Kydren, who was one of Padmasambhava's consorts.)

12. Daughter of Dewa Shakya Raja of Bulbo of Nipal. Her name was Pulmo Shakya Dewa.

13. Daughter of a laborer of Takh, a village near Samyes. Her name is Khando Yeshi Sokgel. (*Note:* This is a strange description of the Queen Yeshe Tsogyal whom King Trisong Deutsen gave to Padmasambhava.)

14. Guru Pudmasumba (Padmasambhava)

15. Pudma Gyelpo

16. Dorjen Lolut

Paralleling the development of Buddhism in Tibet, Bön also evolved from its ancient form into two schools: Eternal Bön (*g yung drung Bön*), a spiritual path with the goal of enlightenment, and New Bön (*bog gsar ma*) developed in conjunction with the secret hidden teachings of tenth- and eleventh-century Tibet, similar to the Nyingma school of Buddhism. Around the tenth century, the advanced knowledge of Bön was formulated into a complex system including teachings delving into magic, funeral ritual, ransom, monastic rules, philosophy, teachings on the great perfection, astrology, psychology, cutting through obstacles, ten precepts for laypeople, primordial sound, how to find a true master and what the commitments are, arts and crafts, logic, medicine, cosmology, and poetry.

At the Tulku Conference in Sarnath in 1988, His Holiness the Fourteenth Dalai Lama stressed the importance of preserving the Bön tradition, as representing the indigenous source of Tibetan culture, and of acknowledging the major role it has had in shaping Tibet's unique identity. He later officially recognized Bön as the fifth Tibetan religious school—alongside the Nyingma, Sakya, Kagyu, and Gelug schools—and has given the Bönpos representation on the Council of Religious Affairs at Dharamsala. Moreover, His Holiness acknowledges that he himself is a holder of the Bön lineage. Given the intertwined heritage of Buddhism and Bön, it is natural that—as we shall see—various aspects of the Cham tradition are derived from the dances of the Bön shamans, a fact attested to by Jamyang Norbu, the former director of the Tibetan Institute of Performing Arts.

All four schools of Tibetan Buddhism use Cham in their rituals, and for all of them, sacred dance is part of the study of a larger system included within Buddhism's tantric practices. The Fifth Dalai Lama tells us that it was the Nyingma school that first established Cham in Tibet, and that they had many different dances derived from visionary dreaming. Guru Rinpoche (Padmasambhava) and other tertons had dreams of dances, remembered what they saw, and handed down their knowledge through the generations, a method that continues today. In the visionary dreams of a modern dance master, Namkhai Norbu—who choreographed a ten-day cycle of dance over a period of three years of dreaming—dakinis came to him at night to make corrections if the steps did not work out properly. The Fifth Dalai Lama in his texts emphasizes the distinction between visionary dreams—considered a valid source of dance choreography—and imagination and daydreaming which are not. The way to distinguish between these two states of mind is explained through restricted or secret teachings.

◾ The Sakya Lineage ◾

SAKYA TRIZAN,
HEAD OF ONE OF THE
FOUR LINEAGES

According to the current Sakya Trizan, the head of the Sakya school, the Sakya lineage was founded because after the persecution of Buddhism by Lang Darma, many tantric ceremonies were being performed for financial gain. Among these ceremonies was the Cham dance. The Khon family, a prominent clan of Nyingma, was horrified by this development and obtained tantric teachings from great masters in India in order to found their own lineage and counteract the corruption. Theirs is the only tradition passed directly from father to son.

17. Nyinma Hotsir
18. Shakya Sange
19. Singe Dadot
20. Lohdun Chukse
21. Nagpa Jhanas. There are fifty of them often dressed alike. When these fifty have gone their round, a sort of play is enacted.
22. The people called Duban who act. Each holds a book, a burlesque of their religious books, in which is an old shoe covered with silk. Placing the real books on the head is regarded as a very solemn ceremony and they seize hold of some of the clowns whose books may be real.
23. The people called Duban disclosing the contents of the book, which instead of being the Kunjur (Kanjur) as they suppose, discover a priapus and an old shoe.
24. Rulmong yak or people playing as musicians. The name of the tent is Chumyur. Chum (Cham) are people who dance before the idols.
25. A pulpit where Lopum Rinpochi reads the Kunjur (Kanjur). It is called Yumbo Chummeti. Yumbo is the name of this tree: *Chumme* (a plain) *ti* (throne).
26. A very ancient pillar, called *doring do* (stone) *ring* (long).

Variations of the dances developed along with the evolution of the different religious schools, divisions within each school, and even each monastery, which might specialize in a particular deity or interpretation of an older dance text. According to Sonam Ridzen, current spokesperson for the Gyuto monks, prior to the Communist Chinese invasion, there were about six thousand monasteries in Tibet, each of them with its own style of Cham. There are special commemorative dances, such as those that celebrate the birth of Tsongkhapa, as well as Chams that reenact historical events or function as empowerments of local guardian deities. Dances also exist outside of Tibet in centers throughout the Himalayan region such as Tashi Jong in India, Rumtek Monastery in Sikkim, in Nepal, and even in the tiny kingdom of Bhutan. Some traditions are barely active, such as the once grand tradition of Cham in Siberian Mongolia.

Cham has its own literature, but this literature is difficult to find because most of it was destroyed by the invasion of Tibet by the Chinese. Much of what was sung, played, and performed in the monasteries was not recorded or even formally written down, while what was preserved has barely been translated into English. Thus it is impossible, when writing about Tibetan dance, to cover the full range of all of the dances from the past to the present. But by exploring some representative dances and the essential elements shared by all Cham dances, it is possible to enter into the profound and magical world of Tibetan sacred dance.

MONKS PRACTICING CHAM IN THE COURTYARD OF RUMTEK MONASTERY, SIKKIM

REPRESENTATIVE CHAMS

SKELETON DANCE

The often performed Skeleton dances are reflective of an important thread of
Tibetan Buddhist wisdom: the teachings of the impermanence of all aspects
of life. Skeletons represent the disintegration of phenomena, including the
body itself, as well as the impermanent nature of various states of mind. The
many variations of the popular Skeleton dances usually belong to one of three
major types. Those depicting monsters or protectors of the cemetery are given
the highest rank. Typically dressed in tight white or red costumes, the dancers
have either three or five little skulls around their head, with rainbow-colored
fans on their ears. In Mongolia they are referred to as butterflies, because of

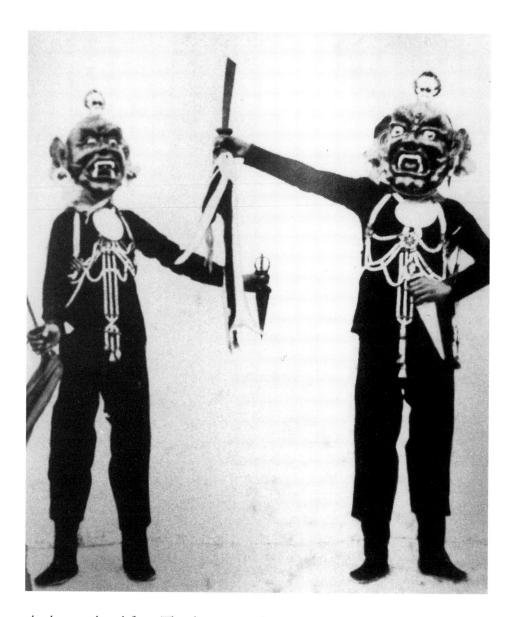

the large colored fans. The dancers in the second type wear masks instead of the rainbow fans. Dressed in patterned pants, they wear white jackets and are supposed to be jokers as well as spirits who bestow luck and riches. The last group are the most rare. They dance holding a stick with a red spiral shape on it and wearing a skull mask.

Skeleton dances are performed in the folk tradition as well as in the monastic tradition. Monks take the roles of both male and female dancers, two of each. The Skeletons are also called *citti patti,* or *tur tu tak ba.* There are also extremely secret Skeleton dances that accompany *chod,* or cemetery practices. These dances are never seen publicly, but are practiced privately in monasteries. They are performed prior to an initiate being sent by his teacher to practice alone in a cemetery or other frightening place. Meditating in a cemetery or in charnel grounds is one of the advanced practices a yogi can do in order to comprehend better the impermanence of all phenomena, including the human body. Many Tibetans and even many Sherpas, mountain guides, have taken initiation into the Chod dances.

The Skeleton dances remind one of an early part of Padmasambhava's epic life story. One day, after his abdication of the throne bequeathed to him by his adopted father, Padmasambhava was dancing on the roof of the palace holding two scepters, one a vajra and the other a trident. As he twirled around, he accidentally dropped the vajra on the head of one of his father's minister's young sons, and the trident pierced the heart of the boy's mother, the minister's wife. Both were killed instantly. Though unintentional, this act was deemed to be murder, and King Indrabhuti—already incensed by Padmasambhava's abdication and other controversial behavior—banished his adopted son to the

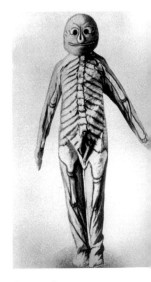

JOKER SKELETON
DANCER

SKELETON
DANCER WITH
RED SPIRAL STICK

MONGOLIAN
SKELETON
DANCER WITH
"BUTTERFLIES"

charnel grounds, where dead bodies were left in the open to decay and be eaten by animals.

This suited Padmasambhava just fine, and he took advantage of his punishment by using human skulls as bricks to construct a meditation temple with eight doors. Padmasambhava later meditated in many cemeteries—including one near Bodhgaya, the site of the Buddha's enlightenment. Although he received many helpful visions from protector spirits, it was not unusual to encounter unfriendly deities during such meditation practice as well. Thus, in the Skeleton dance, Padmasambhava can adopt a wrathful form of nine heads and eighteen arms in order to fend off his attackers.

DEER DANCE

Deer dancers have different meanings depending on the context. When a Deer dancer performs as part of a group, he is one of the many protector deities, and is assigned to cut up the torma offering and rid the new year of negative forces. But when he dances alone, he represents the deer tamed by the eleventh-century Buddhist saint Jetsun Milarepa.

Milarepa, a great mountain yogi, was meditating in his cave when a terrified deer appeared before him. Moved by its fear, he recited verses on the meaning of impermanence. The deer, now calmed, approached him. Then a fierce dog showed up looking for the deer. Milarepa again recited verses on impermanence. The dog became completely tame. Suddenly a hunter named Kyerab Gompo Dorje showed up. He was enraged to see his dog so tame and friendly. The hunter shot an arrow at Milarepa, which fortunately missed. Being an excellent shot, Gompo Dorje realized it was no accident that his arrow missed, and that this yogi was either a saint or a magician. Milarepa again recited his verses on impermanence and the hunter was so moved that he offered up his bow and arrows, his dog, and finally his own body. The dance depicts the deer's gratitude toward Milarepa and appreciation for his newfound friendship with the dog.

This dance is thought to have come from Tser Gontham, a small Kagyu monastery by the Kyichu River. Deer, especially stags, were also very important to the Bön, their antlers often showing up in ancient dismembered offerings.

BLACK HAT DANCE

There are two main traditions of the Black Hat dance, some with seven offerings and others with eight offerings and a mirror. These warriors, or defenders of the dharma, do not wear masks. In the seventeenth century the Fifth Dalai Lama incorporated the Black Hat dance of the Sakya tradition into Namgyal Monastery. Although the dance had been done there since the time of the Fourth Dalai Lama, he gave it a distinctive spin, introducing the "Purba Cham," a longer series with not just one dancer, but rather a group of Black Hat dancers. He also wrote about some of the symbolism of the dance, saying that the hat itself represents the whole world we inhabit with its innate empty nature, while the hat's dome stands for Mount Meru, the symbolic sacred mountain and center of the world. The threads of the hat's fabric are woven in five colors and webbed to eight points in a wheel-like shape, symbolizing the eight minor and major continents. However, the symbolism of the Black Hat dance done in Bhutan, Bodanath, Nepal, and eastern Tibet is not consistent with this explanation.

While this dance is usually regarded as a celebration of the demise of Lang Darma—an enemy of Buddhism who had reinstated the influence of the Bön religion—some debate this point, and the Bön even claim the dance as their own. The dance is also understood as a symbolic depiction of the power of meditation practice to slay our mental afflictions.

WRATHFUL DEITY ON TOP OF A BLACK HAT
SYMBOLIZING THE PROTECTOR ENERGY THAT
GUARDS THE *DHARMA*

Who Was the Black Hat Dancer?

In 772 C.E. King Trisong Deutsen—grateful for his guru Padmasambhava's success in establishing Samye Monastery—offered one of his wives, the remarkable Yeshe Tsogyel, to Padmasambhava as his tantric consort. A year later, by the time she was sixteen, she had received full initiation into the tantras from Padmasambhava. However, when the word got out to the Bön court ministers that the king had scandalously given his queen to the "vagrant sadhu" (wandering ascetic), there was an uproar. Although the king remained confident enough to continue building monasteries and hermitages for Buddhist practice, and ordered that any opposition to himself or Padmasambhava be punished, in order to appease the Bön factions he banished both Padmasambhava and Tsogyel in 774 C.E. and wisely chose as their place of exile the cave Tidrom, northeast of Lhasa, so they could practice meditation.

The Bön court ministers took advantage of Padmasambhava's absence to try to regain their power. Through their machinations, many of the 108 translators

of the Buddhist scriptures appointed by Padmasambhava were banished to outlying districts on one flimsy pretense or another. In order to keep a harmonious court, the king decided it would be best to compromise and give the Bön equal religious status with Buddhism. Thus recognized, the Bön founded their own monastery, called Böngsu, in the Yarlung Valley.

By 776 C.E. Padmasambhava had returned to Samye. At his request, Yeshe Tsogyel went to Nepal to find the Bhutanese girl Tashi Khyidren, who was to become his "awareness dakini" consort. When Tashi Khyidren arrived, Padmasambhava gave her the secret teachings of Vajrakilaya, likening their power to that of receiving an "all protecting escort." Yeshe Tsogyel then begged to receive the Vajrakilaya initiation herself. Padmasambhava agreed to Tsogyel's request and went so far as to tell her that the Vajra Purba was her personal deity. But he also told her that to practice the Vajrakilaya tantra she would need a special consort of her own, a fourteen-year-old boy whom she would find in Uru in central Tibet. Yeshe Tsogyel located the boy identified by Padmasambhava as a special holder of knowledge of the Vajrakilaya initiation. His name, Dudel Pawo,

meant "Devil Destroying Buddha Hero." He was also called Pelgyi Senge or Atsara Sale. However, it is not clear from the myriad accounts if Pelgyi Senge was indeed Atsara Sale or the brother of Yeshe Tsogyel.

Using one of the magical powers of a true tantric adept, Padmasambhava projected wrathful forms of himself all over the land in order to protect the dharma. He transformed himself into the wrathful Dorje Trolo (Diamond-like Sagging Belly) and duplicate forms with names like "Blue-Black Vajra Wrathful Purba" and "Purple Vajra Wrathful Purba."

According to legend, an evil spirit called a *naga* (serpent) living in Lake Manasarovar managed to evade the all-pervading qualities of the Purple Vajra Wrathful Purba. Through magic he transformed himself into a red ox with his feet bound by iron chains and a horrific wound on his head oozing blood and brains. With his tongue lolling and distended and his eyes bulging, he threw himself at King Trisong Deutsen's feet and begged for mercy.

The king, being a very compassionate man, was deeply moved and granted the red ox sanctuary. The ox abruptly vanished, leaving the king completely perplexed. Suddenly he heard the sound of Padmasambhava's voice in his ear, saying

"Your Sympathy is sadly misplaced, O Emperor!
Now in all your future existences
Siddhis will always be fraught with obstacles.
The Buddha's future followers will have
short lives and ill-luck;
In the third generation, this red-ox demon
Transformed into a prince called
Ox (Lang Darma)
Will kill his brother and establish an
iniquitous regime,
Eradicating even the names of sutra and tantra.
However, this is karma and cannot
be deflected."[9]

Pelgyi Senge heard Padmasambhava's words and spontaneously begged for permission to be able to destroy the Ox King. Padmasambhava granted his request and decreed through prophecy that Pelgyi Senge would be the one to kill the Ox King. As this would happen only after three generations, Padmasambhava gave Pelgyi Senge all the initiations and empowerments he would need, along with the special name of Pelgyi Dorje. In due time, the reincarnated Pelgyi Dorje killed Lang Darma after dancing before him, an event symbolically enacted with each performance of the Black Hat dance.

GANDEN SHARTSEN MONKS PERFORMING THE BLACK HAT DANCE IN NEW YORK CITY

MI TSERING
OR TSAGHAN
EBUGEN OF
MONGOLIA,
THE OLD
WHITE MAN

OLD WHITE MAN
FROM A PERFORMANCE
IN INDIA

OLD WHITE MAN FROM MONGOLIA

The performer in the Old White Man dance is dressed in a flowing gown with a mask and walking stick. Symbolically killing a tiger by hitting a tiger skin with his walking stick, he regains the power of his youth and goes on to dance more and more energetically. He is allowed to speak, a privilege other Cham dancers do not have. This dance—derived from a dream the Thirteenth Dalai

Lama had when he fled Tibet into Mongolia—is the youngest dance in the eight-hundred-year history of Tibetan dance. However, Mongol legends also speak of an old white man with a long white beard called Tsaghan Ebugen. Wearing a white robe, possibly a throwback to a shaman's robe, and walking with a dragon-headed staff, he is known as the lord of the mountain who rules the earth and the waters.

MONGOLIAN AND OTHER CHAMS

Cham first entered Mongolia in 1811 through the monastery of Urya[10] and quickly spread to other monasteries. Every Mongolian Buryiat Datsan (abbot) had a special handbook on Chams written in Tibetan or translated into Mongolian from the Tibetan. The form was adapted—lama musicians entered without masks and often danced without musical accompaniment as well. However, the Cham masks did appear and different dances, depending on the theme, were performed. The most popular dances in Mongolia were the Milarepa Chams, Milarepa being the great poet/saint yogi of the Kagyu sect.

In Kathmandu, the Newars, who are Nepali Buddhists, perform Cham in their temples, away from prying eyes. They perform Carya dance, an isolated, rare form of early Indian tantra.

Bu-ston (1290–1364)—the great scholar and prolific writer who made translations of the most important texts in Tibet, called the *Kangyur* and *Tengyur*—also composed two Chams, called "The Offering Dance of the Four Mothers" and "Sham-Pa-Ta Dancing." Another dance in his collected works—"Dance Book of the Four Commands"—does not have a title but contains instructions on how to command and subjugate negative forces.

KALACHAKRA, THE WHEEL OF TIME

When Padmasambhava first came to Tibet, King Trisong Deutsen told him that 108 Buddhist temples had been built during the time of Songtsen Gampo but had fallen into ruin because they were so widely scattered. Padmasambhava decided to construct temples in a style that would represent the mythical Mount Meru—the center or *axis mundi* of the world—with its successive continents and satellite islands. He drew a mandala of five buildings and four temples on the ground and meditated on that spot for five days. Ever since, the mandala formation—significant in many Tibetan sacred art forms—has been particularly important in Cham, which is always performed within the confines of a mandala. The word *mandala* itself derives from the Tibetan word *kyilkhor* (*kyil* means center and *khor* is fringe). In a mandala, everything radiates from the center to the fringe, and all of it is represented by a group of circles set into a series of squares.

SEED SYLLABLE OF
THE KALACHAKRA

PAINTING OF
KALACHAKRA
MANDALA FROM
THE DALAI
LAMA'S PERSONAL
CHAPEL,
NAMGYAL
MONASTERY

Four doorways or gates lead to the inner heart of a mandala, each with a different color and meaning, each connected to one of the major ways we tie ourselves to suffering, *samsara*. The gates employ the cardinal directions— west, east, north, and south. The western gate of the mandala is connected with passion in its negative sense, such as being in a codependent relationship in which you become so glued to another person that there is no boundary

MAKING A
KALACHAKRA SAND
MANDALA DURING A
KALACHAKRA
INITIATION

OPPOSITE:
KALACHAKRA DANCERS
PERFORMING THE
DANCE OF THE
CARDINAL DIRECTIONS

between yourself and the other person. The eastern gate symbolizes aggression, such as when you are at war with yourself, or you are tough, allowing no kind of frivolity or softening. The northern gate represents the habit of crazed or paranoid comparison where others always seem better or more capable than you, and, in order to survive, you strive to become superior so that you can crush or overthrow them and emerge triumphant. The south embodies the arrogant pride of the privileged and entitled, of being smugly confident you need nothing. The core reason for all four gates is transmuting unskillful energy into something active and healthy.

The mandala is particularly significant in the Kalachakra dance, which is performed to encourage world peace now and in the future. Except when a touring troupe offers excerpts for the public, the Kalachakra dance performance coincides with a Kalachakra initiation and the construction of a Kalachakra, or "Wheel of Time," sand mandala. The cloth over the sand mandala—built in the days of preparation before the initiation—is drawn aside only when the vajra dance master recites the mantra of the guard of the eastern gate.

After entering from the east, the dancers circumambulate and make prostrations at each gate, but they do this wearing symbolic blindfolds so they don't actually see the mandala. The monks move in a counterclockwise direction, and make a different offering at each of the four entrances. When they reach a gate, they pause, prostrate, make an offering, then move on to the next gate. At each gate, through their visualization, the buddha, bodhisattva (an enlightened being who gives up attaining *nirvana* to help others), or teacher before whom they prostrate dissolves into them. They first prostrate to the blue buddha Akshobya, who made a vow of compassion to help all sentient beings by purifying their negative actions and emotional patterns. Then they prostrate before the black or green bodhisattva Amoghasiddhi, who represents the air element and grants magical powers *(siddhis)* and fearlessness.

Circumambulating slowly to the southern gate, they prostrate to yellow Ratnasambhava, the "jewel-born" one who rules over the earth and works with feelings. He represents the transformation of pride into equanimity. At this point they are now able to confer the initiation. The dancers circumambulate to the northern gate and transform into white Amitabha, the buddha of boundless light, which allows them to turn the wheel and teach the dharma. Last, they circumambulate to the western gate and transform into yellow Vairochana, one of Tibet's greatest scholars and translators. The dance is completed when all the gates have been visited and all the offerings completed. After the dancers take various vows, they are allowed to remove their symbolic blindfolds and gaze upon the mandala.

The Venerable Lobsang Samten—the ritual dance master of Namgyal Monastery—has likened performing the Kalachakra dances to doing tai chi or walking meditation. The monks often have to balance their entire body on one foot, focusing within their core to gain the necessary physical stability. Their bodies form a three-pronged shape called the Vajra step, which connects the dancers directly to the environment. When the dance is performed, it is difficult to see the dancers' intricate movements under their elaborate costumes made of lengthy layers of brocade. Sometimes the costumes take on a life of their own, swirling after the movement has ceased. The monks must keep their body aligned through all this motion as if a string was pulling them straight up. Though the Vajra step remains unseen, the monks carefully practice it in the sand at their monastery to make sure the three prongs are enacted in the right order and pattern to evoke the inner meaning of the step—sealing the positive energy that the blessing sequence has bestowed.

CHAM GAR

Gar is a type of Cham dance performed only in secret for the lamas themselves. Gar is a tranquil style consisting mostly of hand movements, while Cham is more wrathful and energetic, concentrating more on footwork. The Fifth Dalai Lama said, "When chiefly the hands move, this is called gar, and when mainly the feet move this is known as chams. When mainly both these move this is called 'stang stabs.'"[11] As a style, Gar is also used in other Cham dances, as well as being the name of a type of Achi Lhamo performance, which should not be confused with sacred Gar.

TANTRIC RITUAL
IMPLEMENTS

INITIATION
OFFERINGS

ESSENTIAL ELEMENTS OF CHAM

PREPARATION AND INITIATION

Cham is performed according to the calendar and phases of the moon, whether waxing or waning, with the waning moons traditionally considered inauspicious. A monastery's wealth or a sponsor's financial donations can influence when and how a dance is performed. Other factors are the availability of dance texts, how well trained the dancers are, if the village is obscure or influential, or whether the dance is being performed for the merit of the donor or to fulfill a specific obligation for the community. Some dances must be done only before the creation of a sand mandala and others afterward. Good weather used to be vital since most dances were held outside. In Tibet, weather makers predicted and did practices to control the weather making sure the performances could occur at auspicious times.

Three weeks before a performance, costumes and masks are taken out of storage, fixed, and refitted. A dance rehearsal is held to make sure dancers move easily and can change their costumes in a quick, synchronized flow. Often a *thangka,* a large embroidery with iconography relating to the theme of the dance, is hung over a wall or ledge, or even unfurled down the side of a mountain.

The Cham dancers will be only those monks who have been given the correct initiations *(abhisheka),* allowing them to practice for the sake of all sentient beings. The Sanskrit *abhisheka* means literally "to sprinkle," and an abhisheka is an empowerment in which sacred substances are "sprinkled" upon one's head. Different empowerments are performed according to different levels of spiritual accomplishment, the idea akin to that of turning a prince into a king and a king into a god. Flask empowerments clean impurities in the veins. Secret empowerments clean one's speech. Wisdom empowerments clear the mind, fostering the state of clarity and emptiness. Receiving abhisheka is critical. Only if you have the correct empowerment are you authorized to practice that specific tantra by the teacher.

SYMBOLS FOR AN
ABHISHEKA

Cham dancers also have to be thoroughly instructed. According to Lobsang Samten, "It takes a long time to learn these dances. Just to learn the Blessing of the Ground, one part of the Kalachakra dance, takes three years." In pre-Communist Tibet, monks were taught many different styles and had to pass dance examinations, especially at Namgyal Monastery. Before the Tibetan New Year (falling from December through March according to the lunar calendar), the monks had to perform certain sections of a dance from memory.

THREE MAIN PHASES OF CHAM PERFORMANCE

Cham performances have three main stages: an introduction and preparation phase, the generation and fulfillment phase, and a conclusion. During the introduction and following the dance's conclusion, the dancers practice meditation and invoke the wish to benefit all sentient beings. In the setting up of the dance, and in the slow dancing used to enter and consecrate the mandala,

the distinction between meditation and the post-meditation experience blurs. The heart becomes more compassionate and accommodates the world as it is. That is why Avalokiteshvara, the god of compassion, has one hundred thousand arms, to accommodate all the world's suffering. If the dancers do not meditate for the good of others, the dance becomes just common play and not a transformative meditation practice. This is especially important for Western audiences to understand, because what they are usually seeing at a public venue is an abbreviated part of a larger ritual cycle, outside of its normal cultural context. Traditionally, a dance can include up to seventeen different sections and take all day, or even days, to perform.

The main part of a Cham begins with initiations of earth, wind, water, and fire. In the early stage of the dance, visualization concentrates and stabilizes the mind. Usually these visualizations are of deities called *yidams,* considered to be aspects of the Enlightened One (the Buddha). Sometimes these deities represent positive qualities such as divine pride, clarity, emptiness, and meditation. Even deities that appear wrathful are aids to protecting and propagating the teachings. Many images of protectors proliferate in the Tibetan arts of painting, sculpture, and appliqué, as well as dance. Each of the many types of buddhas and protectors—who vary according to the monastery—

must be approached correctly. For many people in Tibet, these yidams and wisdom spirits are not imaginary beings, but actual, real presences who are pleased when you make offerings to them, an idea that carries traces of shamanism. More sophisticated practitioners see them as manifestations of karma that has not been liberated from its negative influences.

The Tibetan word *yidam* translates as a "promise or pledge to merge." In visualizing the yidam there are two stages, the creation (generation) stage and the fulfillment (perfection) stage. Wisdom beings descend upon the dancer during the creation stage, as the dancer generates the yidam from his stability of mind, and then visualizes his body as the yidam, his speech as mantra, and his mind as clarity, emptiness, and luminosity. After the dancer visualizes himself as the yidam, he visualizes the yidam in front, looking back at him. During the phase of the dance when the yidam is invoked, practitioners assume the disposition of the deity, whether wrathful, semi-wrathful, or peaceful.

In its traditional form, this section can contain as many as eleven different parts. An offering of *chang* (barley beer) is spilled onto the ground to bless it while the dancers enter the performing arena. The musicians are also asked to perform offerings. Dance circles are outlined with chalk or flour. The Dorje Lopon—Thunderbolt Religious Master, sometimes a retired dance master— looks on to make sure that the ceremony is performed correctly. Helpers and up to a hundred musicians march into the performing area to sit in the front rows.

The dancers then circumambulate clockwise to create the form of a sacred mandala. This seals the boundaries against negative energy and empowers the consecrated space. Enemies of the dharma are blocked and the protectors invited inside the protected area. The ground is then blessed again. Dancers move in a clockwise direction, forming two concentric circles. Tall poles fly insignias of the highest-ranking deity with its accompanying colors. These poles or "trees"—also used in Siberian shaman rituals—are seen as a direct link joining heaven and earth to man.

Often an effigy of a corpse represented by a barley cake (torma) is placed in the middle of the circle. First it is examined and attempts are made to destroy it. Then it becomes a food offering for the wrathful and peaceful deities. A feast is prepared and different protectors are invited; peaceful ones are seated on the right and wrathful ones on the left. Invisible buddhas and

THE YIDAM AVALOKITESHVARA WITH 100,000 COMPASSIONATE ARMS

TIBETAN SACRED DANCE

bodhisattvas are seated in the middle. The deities are attracted by *mudras* (hand gestures), the sweet sounds of the bells and drums, and delicious foods. After the feast, the leftovers are gathered and offered to the lesser spirits. Sometimes a wrathful deity *(lingka)* is symbolically struck with the *purba* (a three-bladed kilya knife). To kill the lingka means to kill ignorance and purify it. Sometimes animals are led into a Cham. If they tremble, the gods are happy, a belief that is seen as having shamanistic roots.

Dances can go on all day, though it is rare for a performance to last into the night. Ancillary dancers fill in to play smaller instruments in between the main performing sessions. And then there are always *atsaras* (clowns), roving about and providing humorous interludes by feigning emotions of fear and revulsion.

MANDALA AND MANTRA

In the Indo-Tibetan system of thought, a mandala actually maps the mind and consciousness. It is the psychological diagram of a person in which all of one's experiences are part of one's own unique mandala, or web of consciousness. A nation also has its own mandala, its own shared body of important, central knowledge and fringe information. At the same time, within any country, state, or region there are collective and individual mandalas that overlap one another.

POSSIBLE MANDALA
DATING FROM 700 TO
800 C.E.

STATE ARTIST OF
BHUTAN PAINTING
A MANDALA

DANCE OF THE
"FAIRIES" (DAKINIS)
AT SERTRENG
CEREMONY, LHASA,
APRIL 1921.
PHOTO BY SIR
CHARLES BELL

ANCIENT
REPRESENTATION
OF A *MANDALA*
CIRCLE

The symbolism of the mandala circle used in Cham functions simultaneously on three levels. The first level represents a home for the realm of the gods, one of the six realms of existence (for the gods, jealous gods, humans, animals, hungry ghosts, and hell). The second level of function is its own physical location on earth, which includes its representation of Mount Meru.

At the third level the mandala functions within the physical body of a Cham dancer or other tantric practitioner as the secret centers known as *chakras*. In that, the head and four limbs of a person symbolize Mount Meru and the four continents. The eyes are the sun and the moon. The body itself is where the deity lives. The orifices are the entrances into the mandala. This outline also corresponds to the meeting of the nerve clusters in the body, which are called *nadis*. Concentration and meditation techniques are specifically taught through oral instructions passed from tantric masters to their students. These practices open and purify the chakras to overcome negative obstacles, to counteract the work of negative karma, and to achieve what Buddhists call enlightenment. The Cham dancer concentrates on all of these centers during a performance in which even the smallest gesture is part of the monk's practice of unifying body, speech, and mind.

Mantras—part of a secret oral tradition—are recited while the monks dance in order to interrupt habitual thinking and keep the mind from dwelling on its usual stream of thought. The ancient texts say the mantras should be said "in a hissing way, with the teeth pressed against each other."[12] Recitation of texts that instruct in visualizations, mantra, music, and praise can take more time to complete than the dance itself.

DANCE STEPS AND MUDRAS

In Cham, the body postures of the dancers are specified down to their most exacting detail, with all the foot, hand, and body movements representing qualities of the deities (yidams). Even the method of donning ritual clothing is specified. In order to pick up their costumes, the dance practitioners must lift them from the right side and then switch, putting on clothes over their head exclusively from the left side.

NAMGYAL MONKS PERFORMING DANCE STEPS WITH ACCOMPANYING *MUDRAS* DURING A KALACHAKRA INITIATION

Many of the steps have specific names such as "Half-thunderbolt," "Wide Lotus," "Leaping Lotus," and "Move Walk." An instruction from the Fifth Dalai Lama's *Chams Yig* illustrates the exact nature of the Chams dance techniques: "Then lifting the right foot one puts it towards the left; lifting the left one, one sets it in front, and lifting the left foot one sets it towards the right. This form is called 'Leaping Lotus.'"[13] There are also both masculine and feminine ritual parts that vary according to the dance.

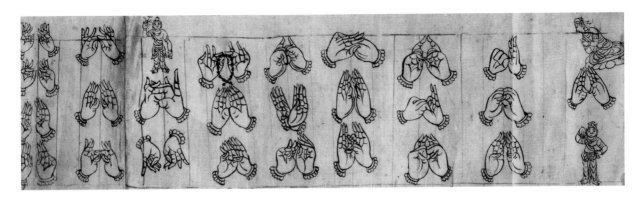

The torso is held straight in Cham dance, as is the waist. Fingers usually curl inward when the knee is raised. When the knee comes down, so does the finger, and the thumb curls in toward the palm. When the foot lands, it is symbolic of wisdom blending with compassion. Once these movements are mastered, the dancer does not need to dwell on the specifics, but needs only to retain the yidam visualization.

The *mudras* (hand gestures) used in Cham originated in India, where—according to Indian traditions—mudras are gestures that portray the correct way to treat a guest. The eight most common mudras are: 1) *argam,* invitation; 2) *pande,* falling water or, from older times, washing the feet; 3) *pushpe,* flower; 4) *dupe,* incense; 5) *aloke,* lamp; 6) *gande,* mirror; 7) *rasa,* taste; and 8) *shabde,* sound. Snapping the fingers in the context of a mudra represents either the sound of emptiness or the interdependent nature of all sound. The thumb and pointer finger on one's hand represent wisdom and compassion, while all ten fingers are symbolic of wind or wind energy. According to the tantric system, wind and consciousness of mind always flow together. Wind is like a horse and consciousness is mind energy that rides the horse. Through control of the wind energy, one gains control of the entire subtle nervous system.

Hand mudras or gestures change according to the subtlety of the tantric level practiced. The higher the tantric level, the more subtle the gesture until ultimately they function only at the mental level. This is why some of the highest initiations, such as the Kalachakra, contain the slowest and most subtle forms of the dance.

CHAM DANCERS ENTERING COURTYARD,
BHUTAN. PHOTO BY CHÖGYAM TRUNGPA

MUDRAS FROM A CAVE AT DUN-HUANG. TANG DYNASTY, LATE 9TH CENTURY C.E. INK ON PAPER. FROM THE COLLECTION OF THE BRITISH MUSEUM

EXAMPLE OF A *MUDRA.* CENTRAL ASIAN STATUE FROM THE HERMITAGE MUSEUM, ST. PETERSBURG, RUSSIA

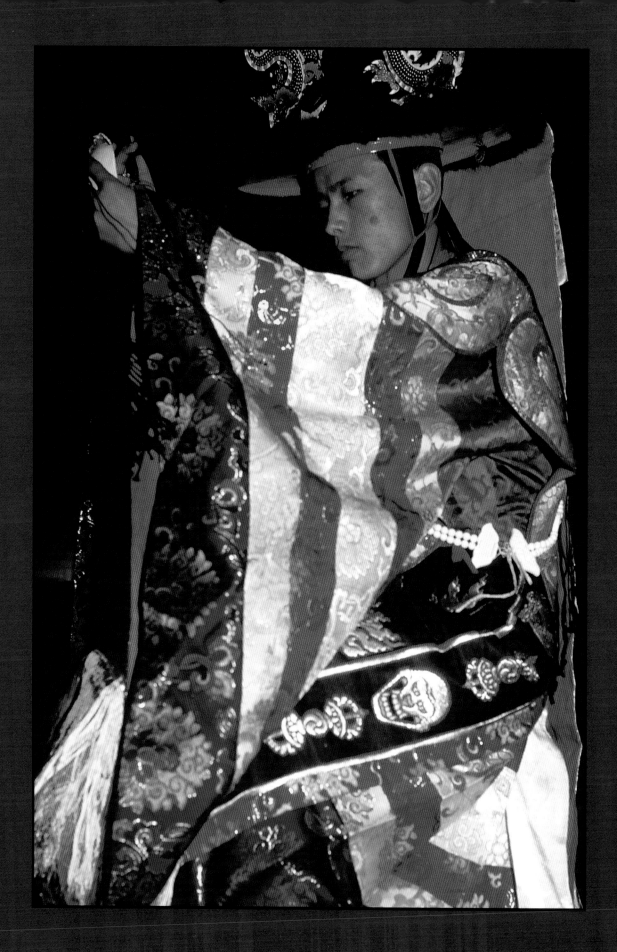

COSTUMES

Like the dance steps, the colorful brocade costumes in Cham dance are highly symbolic, containing double and triple meanings. The significance of the colors used for the costumes, flags, tapestries, and other fabrics of Cham dance can change according to region or lineage. However, the most common meanings of the colors are as follows:

Red = fire, energy, power
White = water, peace
Yellow = earth, increase, growth
Green = air (having limits)
Blue = space (limitless)
Black = wrath

ILLUSTRATIONS OF THE DIVERSITY OF CHAM COSTUMES

SEWING COSTUMES, THE TIBETAN INSTITUTE OF PERFORMING ARTS, DHARAMSALA, INDIA

OPPOSITE: BROCADE COSTUME OF BLACK HAT DANCER

69

SPINNING THREAD,
DHARAMSALA

OPPOSITE: TAILOR
PUTTING FINISHING
TOUCHES ON THE RIBS
OF A SKELETON
DANCE COSTUME

Dance costumes are a blend of Indian pantomime costumes from medieval Indian monasteries and Tibetan-style clothes. The *Chams Yig* details appropriate attire, especially for the Vajrakilaya and Black Hat dances. It says, "The lower part of the dancing garment should move as when the great eagle soars to heaven; the locks [hair] should be shaken like the rising 'lion with the turquoise locks'; the grace of the body should be like that of an Indian tiger stretching himself gracefully in the forest."[14] The book discusses a specific gown called a *phod ka* that hangs down to the ankles. It is indigo blue or black and extensively embroidered. The sleeves are wide, funnel shaped, and embroidered in bright shades of red and yellow.

TIBETAN SACRED DANCE

The dancers often wear wigs made of either human or yak hair and multicolored silk ribbons. Other parts of the costume can be felt boots and a poncholike cloak embroidered and lined with silk. Clothing of the dakas (male deities) and dakinis (female deities) is similar, but the dakini costumes are more feminine.

The dancers wear various bone ornaments such as bracelets, anklets, and an apron. In the past, the ornaments were carved from real human bone. Sometimes the apron has interlinked meshlike carved plates of dakini pictures strung together with round beads. It may be beautifully embroidered with a three-eyed wrathful figure, or may hold ashes from a cremated corpse that the dancer spreads on his body. Dancers also may wear wood or bone breast ornaments the size of grapefruit.

DAKINI DANCER
HOLDING SKULL
CUP AND *VAJRA*

DANCERS
WEARING BONE-
ORNAMENT
APRONS

Sometimes the bone ornaments display secret seed syllables, Indian Sanskrit letters that have been adapted into Tibetan script. A seed syllable represents a basic primordial sound such as "AH" that is used as an object of contemplation. They also represent subtle flows of energy and it is said enlightened beings emanate from these syllables. Gazing at the syllables is a powerful form of meditation. Each part of the five-spoked crown of a dakini dancer contains a seed syllable representing one of the five Buddha families and its respective color.

The performers also carry various ritual objects in some of the dances. The *Chams Yig* mentions a mirror—a tantric symbol for the nature of unobscured mind—surrounded by peacock feathers. The handbell represents wisdom and compassion. The dorje, or diamond thunderbolt scepter, represents compassion and skillful means. Symbolic weapons such as purbas, vajras, and dorjes usually have fluttering scarves attached to them. In the masked drum dances *(rnga),* dancers carry drums and curved sticks with which they beat out a harsh rhythm.

MASKS

Masks are not viewed as inanimate objects, but are believed to actually embody the deity (yidam) they represent. Most masked figures have only one face. The highest-ranked wrathful deities have a tiara ringed with five skulls. The lower the rank of the deity, the fewer the number of skulls in the tiara. All masks must be consecrated through the use of mantras and the throwing of offering rice before they are considered ready. They are locked up in a special room inside the monastery when not in use. If they last a long time they are considered extremely sacred. Interpreted on a higher level, the masks symbolize the illusion that conceals the innate underlying reality of emptiness.

Masks are made of wood, papier-mâché, brass, or copper. Masks of copper with a third eye are used in dance only during the most important ceremonies. Much of the face is uncovered and a huge earring hangs down the side of the head.

THE HIGHEST-
RANKED MASKS
HAVE THE MOST
SKULLS IN THE
TIARA.

75
◨
TIBETAN SACRED DANCE

MASK MOLD

PREPARING
THE EYES OF
THE MASK

◘ Making a Mask ◘

Clay or papier-mâché masks are constructed with the use of a mold. To make a clay mask, the clay must be wet and pounded to make it malleable. Yak glue is boiled and mixed together with the clay. The eyes, jaw, forehead, and other facial contours are sculpted around a dome or triangle, sized to allow the dancer to gaze out through the nostrils of the mask. If appropriate, a band of skulls is placed along the forehead. The mask is dried for three to four days in the sun on top of a roof, with the hope that the clay will not crack as it dries. After it is dry, a paintbrush is used to brush cloth strips cut into triangles inside the mold to make a cushion for the person who will wear the mask. Each layer is allowed to dry before another layer is placed on top of it. When it is thick enough, a mallet is used to hit the mold and knock the mask out from inside of it. The remaining clay is scraped off. Fine clay is mixed with cotton to render details like eyebrows and teeth. It is left to dry once again in the sun and then painted with colorful tempera paint. After the mask is fully painted, shellac or polyurethane is put over it to seal and waterproof the work. These last steps vary from the older ways to make masks, as tradition has adapted to the introduction of modern techniques.

CONTOURING THE EYES OF THE MASK

CHARACTERS

Cham dances feature various characters, most of which fall under the following types: 1) gods of the Tibetan pantheon; 2) *tramen,* goddesses or witches; 3) *ging,* low-ranked gods; 4) *mahakalas,* or wrathful protectors; 5) clowns and jokers called atsaras; 6) mythical characters; and 7) humans.

The gods can be one of the eight *Dharmapalas,* Guardians of the Law:

> Yama, the lord of death, who has the head of a water buffalo and always wears an ornament shaped like a wheel on his breast
>
> Mahakala, the wrathful black protector, personal deity of Kublai Khan
>
> Yamantaka, a fierce emanation of Manjusri, the god of wisdom, who resembles Yama but has eight arms and legs
>
> Kubera or Vaisravana, the god of wealth
>
> Hayagriva, the horse-necked one, a wrathful manifestation of Avalokiteshvara, the god of compassion
>
> Palden Lhamo, the only female among the eight protectors, a protectress of the Dalai Lama and Buddhist governments
>
> Tshangs pa, or "White Brahma"
>
> Begtse, the god of war, the last to appear among the eight, from Mongolia, said to symbolize the conversion of the Mongols to Buddhism

PALDEN LHAMO
IN A PROCESSION

Palden Lhamo (Glorious Goddess), the main wrathful goddess of the Tibetan pantheon, is a familiar figure in many Cham dances. Thangkas portray her crossing a sea of blood on her mule, riding sideways atop the flayed corpse of her own son. Palden Lhamo killed her own son so that his father, her husband, a fierce warrior, would feel the pain his murders were causing others and stop his killing. It shows she would do anything to achieve peace. Palden Lhamo is

easily recognized. She is dark blue with three eyes, a gaping mouth, and sharp teeth that crunch human corpses. Palden Lhamo's forehead has a diadem, a crescent moon, five skulls, and a peacock feather, and her hair rises up in flames. In her right hand is either a sword or a mummified corpse, and in her left hand is a skull cup filled with blood and brains. The snow lion and sea monster are part of her entourage of wrathful emanations.

Also frequently portrayed is Yama, the god of death, with his sisters, Yami and Camundi. Sometimes Yama is accompanied by eight male and eight female companions. Yama is blue, and his mask has three bull's eyes. He also has five skulls, small horns, a club in the shape of a mummified corpse, and a noose in his left hand. He has different emanations: Yama of the east with a white mask; Yama of the south, who is yellow; Yama of the west, who is red; and Yama of the north, who is blue.

OPPOSITE: WRATHFUL PROTECTOR OF CHAM

PAINTING OF PALDEN LHAMO, PROTECTRESS OF HIS HOLINESS THE DALAI LAMA AND THE TIBETAN STATE

Dorje Trollo, one of the wrathful but ultimately benevolent forms of Padmasambhava, is represented with a large brown mask with five skulls. His eyes bulge, his fangs are enormous, and his hair is made out of a yak's tail. He wears a tunic with a crossed vajra and sports a large earring with a wheel. Holding a ribboned vajra in his right hand and a purba in his left, he symbolically stabs in all directions, and then stabs at a torma, which he "eats."

Tramen, on the other hand, are goddesses or little witches with a sexy appealing body and the face of an owl, dog, raven, pig, sea monster, snow lion, tiger, yak, wolf, or crow. Animal images serve as guardians of the mandala, as attendants of a mahakala protector deity and have links to shamanic times. Some derive from the Bön tradition and some from vedic India. The tramen dance naked and often carry weapons in their hands, using a lasso, hook, chains, and bells. They are symbolic of the four karmas—pacifying, magnetizing, enriching, and destroying—and also represent the four enlightened qualities of compassion, equanimity, joy, and love.

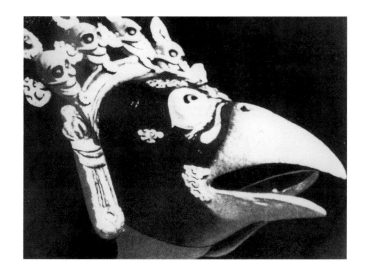

TOP: DORJE TROLLO, SEA MONSTER (*MAKARA*)
MIDDLE: DOG, OLD WOMAN
BOTTOM: GARUDA, WILD YAK
RIGHT: CROW OR RAVEN
OPPOSITE: GING, BEATING A DRUM

DIFFERENT FORMS OF
MAHAKALAS

Ging are also a throwback to the Bön tradition, representing all sorts of spirits from the different realms, both male and female. Ging are also thought of as the special emissaries of Padmasambhava. Lighthearted and sweet, they make everyone laugh. Performing in sets of four, eight, and sixteen, they play their drums as they dance toward one another in pairs, then turn back to back when they can't get any closer.

Different forms of mahakalas, or wrathful demons, appear frequently. Tibetan iconography chronicles between seventy-two and seventy-five mahakalas, each of whom has up to six female consorts.

Atsaras are jokers or clowns who are ever present and frolic about, even during solemn moments in a ceremony. *Atsara* is a corruption of the Sanskrit word *acarya*, which means "spiritual teacher." There are male and female atsaras. Some have dark hair or are bearded with long hair in a topknot and have big noses. They are the only ones who are allowed to joke about the dharma, because hidden beneath their clowning is an implied reference to the truth of the nature of perception, and the fact that the monks can know it but cannot portray it. If a Cham dancer's mask becomes crooked or a costume comes undone, the atsaras jump in to fix it. They are also used for crowd control and to collect donations.

GARUDA, THE DEADLY ENEMY OF THE *NAGA* SNAKE CREATURES. A SPECIAL GARUDA CHAM WAS TRADITIONAL TO COMMEMORATE THE DEATH OF THE FIFTH DALAI LAMA'S REGENT, DESI SANGYE GYATSO.

HO SHANG

OPPOSITE:
ONE OF FOUR
MYTHICAL KINGS,[15]
YUK HORSUNG,
KING OF THE
EAST, PURE AS
A SNOW WHITE
MOUNTAIN,
PLAYING A
STRINGED
INSTRUMENT.
OUTER WALL
RUMTEK
MONASTERY,
SIKKIM

MACHIG
LABDROM
PLAYING BELL
AND *DAMARU*

One of the most commonly seen mythical creatures is a Garuda. Garudas have birdlike attributes and are considered to be deadly enemies of *nagas,* or snake creatures. They represent the quality of outrageousness and are said to fly free once they hatch from their eggs.

Hashang (Ho Shang in Chinese) is a Chinese man who shows up often in Tibetan Cham dance as a figure of ridicule, stemming from eighth-century Tibetan history. Sometime after the establishment of Samye Monastery by Padmasambhava, King Trisong Deutsen, and Shantarakshita, tensions arose due to vast differences in interpretation and translation between Chinese and Indian versions of Buddhist scriptures. In 792 Trisong Deutsen declared a public debate held at Samye to decide which course of scriptural interpretation should be used, Indian or Chinese. Shantarakshita's most prominent student, Kamalashila, made the difficult journey from Nalanda University in India in order to argue the Indian point of view, which was that the path to liberation existed in certain defined stages and that enlightenment was attainable only through practice and achieving merit. The Chinese emperor's representative, the monk Ho Shang, argued that the Ch'an (which is best known now as its Japanese derivative the Zen school) relied very much on "no thought," with emptiness and enlightenment being attained in a flash—known in the West as the *satori* experience. Kamalashila won the debate and in C.E. 799 the king officially declared the Indian interpretation of Buddhism the state religion. As the loser of the debate, Ho Shang is always depicted in a comic or derogatory light.

MUSIC

In all early cultures, music served ritual. Before Buddhism entered Tibet, Bön music used to accompany ritual chanting to communicate with supernatural forces, invoking benevolent spirits and exorcising evil ones. Tibetan music is both devotional and symbolic. Devotional music is directed toward a specific lama or deity. Symbolic music is where every sound from an animate or inanimate object is usable. For example, the human thighbone is an instrument with mystical properties, serving as a symbol of mortality and impermanence. The function of music in Tibetan religious ceremonies is always directed toward the attainment of enlightenment.

Songs are called dakini melodies because the female (dakini) sound is considered to be prettier than the male (daka) sound. A particular phrase might have one set meaning at the basic level of practice and another meaning at a more advanced stage. The natural voice itself is called *rang-skad* and the diphthonic, or more tantric syllabic chanting, is called *mdzo-skad*. Tibetan Buddhist monks are famous for producing deep bass notes that come from relaxing their vocal chords to resonate an octave below the note that is normally sung. The chanting is embellished with a prolonged *glissando* that slides up and down from note to note. Another type of chanting, also found in old Arabic traditions, uses the breathing techniques used for playing instruments. The musician breathes in through his nose without any break, using his mouth as a wind reservoir. This allows the sound to keep going for a long time.

Tantric words or seed syllables are always kept secret. Performers like the Gyuto tantric monks, who are well known in the West, chant using various speeds to obscure the tones so the audience cannot clearly ascertain the meaning of the words. For example, they are adept at using the deep tone of the wrathful deity Yamantaka and imitating his voice while hiding the meaning. Very slow chanting allows the monks to ponder the meaning of the words for

MONKS REHEARSING, RUMTEK MONASTERY COURTYARD, SIKKIM

TIBETAN SACRED DANCE

themselves. This type of singing involves a main chant master simultaneously using three notes. Each note by itself creates a complete chord in a type of multiphonic singing known as *jok-kay* (low tone) and *bar-da* (high tone). It is also known as overtone singing, in which the reshaping of the vocal cavity enables the body to become its own amplifier. Monastic chanting further breaks down into three types of vocalization. *Dön* is a plain normal voice used for recitation of texts. *Ta* is patterned melodies and *yang* is the complex overtone singing.

Two types of musical notation are used in Tibetan monasteries, one for vocal and one for instrumental. A musical notation that moves from low to high and goes gradually low again is referred to as a "long melody." A medium notation also exists that is quicker and has fewer vocal changes. A note between a high, middle, and low tone that does not need more than one or two pitch changes is called short. A *dor* is a very deep note, and a *dor-had* is similar but a bit shorter followed by a higher note. A *shung* is a prolonged note of medium pitch, and *ti* is a high note. Notations symbolize all of these changes. Although it is written down in texts called *Dbyangs Yig,* Tibetan notation is not standardized like that of Western music with a bar and scales and chords. It usually sets the tone for the first line of a text, the balance of which is meant to have been memorized. It is used more interpretatively, with the musicians deciding when the music and words dovetail. Tibetan notation is so wide ranging that each lineage and even the largest monasteries have their own systems.

blow three times
(*sum-'bud*)

blow three times
with a rest
(*sum-'bud bcad-ma*)

blow three times
emphatically
(*rgyang gzhol-can*)

blow four times
with a rest
(*bzhi-'bud bcad-ma*)

blow four times
emphatically
(*bzhi-'bud glog-ma*)

a variation of the
preceding notation

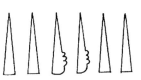

blow six long notes
(*drug-'bud ring-ba*)

MUSICAL INSTRUMENTS

There are seven main types of Tibetan musical instruments.

1. Long trumpets of various sizes such as the enormous twelve-foot *radong,* the instrument most associated with Tibetan music. It provides the basis of any ritual music and is blown continually, its momentous tones ebbing and swelling. The *dung* is another type of long trumpet that plays deep bass calls (often of just one note), either alone or as part of a monastery's orchestra.

2. Wind instruments such as the *rGyaling* (shawm), which is usually used to announce the arrival of a lama or important event, and the *rGaling* or double-reed oboe, which plays melodies, both as part of the monastery orchestra and separately in a repertoire of tunes for special occasions.

3. Handled drums, known as *rGna,* that are supported on a stick or held in a frame and struck with a crooked stick or, occasionally, with drumsticks. They are used for ritual chanting, often to protector deities. The bass drum was especially important in Bön rituals because it talked directly to the demons.

MONKS CARRYING
BASS DRUMS,
SERTRENG FESTIVAL,
1921, LHASA.
CHAKPORI INSTITUTE,
A MEDICAL COLLEGE IS
IN THE BACKGROUND.

4. The conch shell, or *dung-dkar*. Also played alone or with an orchestra, it usually announces the call to an activity.

5. Hand drums called *damaru,* made from either wood or human skulls. A *damaru* is a small drum with a semi-hourglass shape, played by rotation of the right wrist, causing its clappers to strike the drum skin. Played along with a handbell, or *ghanta,* by the same player, they are used in ritual tantric practice to invite the deities. A damaru, called a *nga,* was originally used by Bön priests.

6. Thighbone trumpet or *rKangling,* a short horn sometimes made from metal but usually from a human thighbone. It is used alone or for specialized rituals, especially for chod practice.

7. Cymbals of various types. The *drilbu,* or handbell, is held in the left hand and played along with a hand drum by the same person. *Rolmo,* larger cymbals held one above the other and struck together vertically, are used during initiations. *Silnyen,* cymbals with no central boss, are struck using horizontal movements, and are also used during initiations. Also played are gongs, *mkar-rnga,* and metal disks, *ting-ting.*

CONCH SHELLS
(DUNG-DKAR)

OVERTONE
CHANTING WITH
CYMBALS

▣ The Dance of the Oracle Protector ▣

When Padmasambhava consecrated Samye Monastery with the Vajrakilaya dance, he tamed the local spirit protector, Pehar Gyalp, and bound him by oath to become the head of the entire hierarchy of Buddhist protective spirits. Pehar, later known as Dorje Drakden, became the principal protector of the Dalai Lamas, manifesting through the Nechung Oracle.

According to the Dalai Lama, "Tibetans rely on oracles for various reasons. The purpose of the oracles is not just to foretell the future. They are called upon as protectors and sometimes used as healers. However, their primary function is to protect the Buddha Dharma and its practitioners.

"In the Tibetan tradition, the word *oracle* is used for a spirit which enters those men and women who act as mediums between the natural and the spiritual realms. The mediums are, therefore, known as *kuten*, which literally means 'the physical basis.'"

In 1947 Lobsang Jigme, the Tibetan State Oracle, prophesied that in the Year of the Tiger, 1950, Tibet would face great difficulty. In 1951, Lobsang Jigme fell ill, some say because of his repeated troubling visions, and for years was unable to walk without assistance. In 1959, after predicting the Dalai Lama's flight, Lobsang Jigme spent two months walking to India with His Holiness. His illness was eventually cured.

In his autobiography, *Freedom in Exile*, His Holiness the Dalai Lama writes:

"Nechung has his own monastery in Dharamsala, but usually he comes to me. On formal occasions, the Kuten is dressed in an elaborate costume consisting of several layers of clothing topped by a highly ornate

ABOVE AND LEFT: PEHAR, THE DALAI LAMA'S ORACLE PROTECTOR

ABOVE: STATE ORACLE OF TIBET FOR THE THIRTEENTH DALAI LAMA IN CHUMI LI VALLEY
BELOW: LOBSANG JIGME, CURRENT STATE ORACLE OF TIBET. PHOTO COURTESY OF LOWELL THOMAS JR.

robe of golden silk brocade, which is covered with ancient designs in red and blue and green and yellow. On his chest he wears a circular mirror which is surrounded by clusters of turquoise and amethyst, its polished steel flashing with the Sanskrit mantra corresponding to Dorje Drakden. Before the proceedings begin, he also puts on a sort of harness, which supports four flags and three victory banners. Altogether, this outfit weighs more than seventy pounds and the medium, when not in trance, can hardly walk in it.

"The ceremony begins with chanted invocations and prayers, accompanied by the urgings of horns, cymbals, and drums. After a short while,

TIBETAN SACRED DANCE

the Kuten enters his trance, having been supported until then by his assistants, who now help him over to a small stool set before my throne. Then, as the first prayer cycle concludes and the second begins, his trance begins to deepen. At this point, a huge helmet is placed on his head. This item weighs approximately thirty pounds, though in former times it weighed over eighty.

"Now the Kuten's face transforms, becoming rather wild before puffing up to give him an altogether strange appearance, with bulging eyes and swollen cheeks. His breathing begins to shorten and he starts to hiss violently. Then, momentarily, his respiration stops. At this point the helmet is tied in place with a knot so tight that it would undoubtedly strangle the Kuten if something very real were not happening. The possession is now complete and the mortal frame of the medium expands visibly.

"Next, he leaps up with a start and, grabbing a ritual sword from one of his attendants, begins to dance with slow, dignified, yet somehow menacing, steps. He then comes in front of me and either prostrates fully or bows deeply from the waist until his helmet touches the ground before springing back up, the weight of his regalia counting for nothing. The volcanic energy of the deity can barely be contained within the earthly frailty of the Kuten, who moves and gestures as if his body were made of rubber and driven by a coiled spring of enormous power.

"There follows an interchange between Nechung and myself, where he makes ritual offerings to me. I then ask any personal questions I have for him. After replying, he returns to his stool

and listens to questions put by members of the government. Before giving answers to these the Kuten begins to dance again, thrashing his sword above his head. He looks like a magnificent, fierce Tibetan warrior chieftain of old.

"As soon as Dorje Drakden has finished speaking, the Kuten makes a final offering before collapsing, a rigid and lifeless form, signifying the end of the possession. Simultaneously, the knot holding his helmet in place is untied in a great hurry by his assistants, who then carry him out to recover whilst the ceremony continues."[16]

CLIMACTIC MOMENT IN A SACRED DANCE

FESTIVALS

Cham dances are often performed as a part of annual celebrations such as the
Gu Tor and Mani Rimdu festivals, in which several Chams are grouped
together. The Gu Tor festival (Day of the Great Discarding of the Torma) has
a day of dance specifically associated with Namgyal Monastery. The day
begins with an invocation to the three jewels—the Buddha, the dharma, and
the sangha. Seven dancers appear in the courtyard with the Chinese monk Ho
Shang and his two children, Ho and Trug. They are followed by two Indian

sadhus (wandering holy ascetics) and then by the two Lords of the Cemetery. First, a dance called *Sa-dul* is performed to carry out the important function of preparing and taming the ground (*sa* translates as "ground" and *dul* is "to subdue or tame"). It is followed by eight preliminary dances with different beats, some slow, some fast, some wrathful, and some peaceful. The Lords of the Cemetery come back to look for the image of a corpse (symbolized by the torma) placed in the center of a circle. Then the dance of the Old White Man occurs, followed by the Black Hat dance.

In the evening, another ritual called a Dep is performed by thirty-four monks who dance together in their everyday robes. Camundi, the female partner of Yama, dances a solo with all others later joining in. This ceremony is done to eliminate obstacles and negative influences, especially those that obstruct the dharma. Tea is poured into a sacred vessel, called the *Ser-kyem* (Gold Libation). It is offered to the head lama, the yidam, and all the dharma protectors to invite them to use their enlightened activity. The monks visualize themselves as different yidams and protectors and approach a representation of a human body visualized as a malevolent force. Nine ritual weapons used to cut through enemies and obstacles are displayed—a sword, hooked knife, noose, iron chain, bell, skull, chopping knife, trident, and dagger. When the dagger is plunged into the torma, its symbolic consciousness leaves and disappears into the pure realm, representing the termination of the mind's suffering and attachment, not the actually killing of anything or anyone.

A young monk then performs the wrathful Deer dance and cuts the torma into pieces, scattering it around. A fire pit off to the side holds boiling oil. A paper effigy is placed above the fire and then a skull cup laden with alcohol is poured deep into the cauldron of hot oil. There is a large explosion, symbolic of the burning of negativities. Pouring the alcohol is extremely dangerous and done only by a skilled and trained monk. The ritual ends with the *lor-cham* (returning dance). The Deer dancer departs first, and all others follow in reverse order from the beginning of the day's festivities. The musicians leave in a formal line, then a prayer ceremony is performed. Close to the sanctified area a hut of dry grass is set on fire and the ritual torma is thrown into it. Then everyone goes home. This is done the last day of the Tibetan year to purify all negativity before the start of the New Year.

Mani Rimdu—a very active festival even in modern times—is held at Tengboche Monastery in the northeast Khumbu area of Nepal, close to Mount Everest. Usually performed on the full moon in the ninth Tibetan month, which falls in late October, it is done to invoke the blessings of Chenrezig (Avalokiteshvara), the god of compassion. *Mani* comes from part of the prayer to Chenrezig and *rimdu* are small blessed red pills given to everyone at the end of the ceremony. Well known for the monks performing the masked dance, it tells the story of how Buddhism came into Tibet. A sand mandala is built over four days, and is used as an object of meditation for ten days. At the end of the ceremony, sixteen Cham dances are interspersed with comic interludes. Many of the Chams show the teachings of Padmasambhava. At the end of the festival a fire ceremony *(puja)* is performed by the monks and the sand mandala is dismantled and dedicated to all sentient beings. The whole village participates in this festival, which is especially important for the local Sherpa community and is on the itinerary of many Western tour and trekking companies.

BURNING OF THE TOR-MA AT THE TOR-GYA, TIBET
1. THE TORMA
2. HUT OF MARSH GRASS IN WHICH TORMA IS BURNT
3. SIMILAR HUT BURNT AT THE SAME TIME (CAPTION AND NOTES BY SIR CHARLES BELL)

PURPOSE AND INTERPRETATION

Tibetan Buddhism categorizes learning into five major and five minor sciences called *rigpa*. The major sciences are: logical analysis, sound, the creative arts, health, and healing. Dance fits in under these definitions as part of both sound and the creative arts. The five lesser sciences are: astrology, metaphor, metrics, the performing arts, and poetry. Both Cham and Achi Lhamo are part of the performing arts. Under the umbrella of dance there are five further subcategories: memorized texts, comedic improvisational performance, display, structure and meaning of costumes, music (including chant), and finally the dance and its numerous representations. These other representations include written descriptions, paintings, and even sketches of the performances themselves.

CHANTING DURING AN INITIATION

Tibetan Cham dance is part of a larger system of tantric practices done for spiritual purposes. Cham dances also serve a secondary purpose more closely aligned with shamanistic practices—to rid a particular village or community of negativity, eradicate disease, and promote bountiful harvests. As Cham dances are performed for the benefit of all sentient beings, the merit from the initiations is shared with others. But this altruism was not always in effect. In the Fifth Dalai Lama's book on sacred dance, written in 1647, he discussed his own dance training, saying, "I myself have trained, practiced and made comments in writing upon [this] dance." He then criticized his contemporaries in a surprisingly sardonic tone: "Nowadays, some priests not knowing anymore the way of practicing correctly the rites of secret mantras perform the dance as they think is suitable only in order to gain food, and in this manner they deceive other people. They think that the 'chams is just like ordinary play and spectacle.'"[17]

The issue surrounding the correct practice and interpretation of sacred dance and music inevitably arose through the rare contact Westerners had with Tibetan culture prior to 1959. When individuals from the West first encountered Tibetan music and dance they were dumbfounded. While visitors who managed to overcome the arduous treks and inhospitable conditions were extremely rare, a few hardy individuals did manage to travel throughout the country. A diary written in 1783 by Captain Samuel Turner—an ambassador to Tibet and an English officer who met the infant Panchen Lama—describes his first encounter with monastic music:

> As far as I am able to judge, respecting their ritual, or ceremonial worship, it differs materially from the Hindoo. The Tibetans assemble in chapels, and unite together in prodigious numbers to perform their religious service, which they chant in alternative recitative a chorus accompanied by an extensive band of loud and powerful instruments so that whenever I heard these congregations, they forcibly recalled to my recollection both the solemnity and sound of the Roman Catholic mass.
>
> The instruments were all of an enormous size, trumpets above six feet long. Drums stretched over a copper cauldron . . . the gong, a circular Chinese instrument of thin hammered bell metal capable of producing a surprising sound . . . cymbals, hautboys, and a double drum, shallow, but of a great circumference, mounted upon a tall, slender pedestal which the performer turns with great facility, striking either side with a curved iron, as the piece requires a higher, or lower tone. These, together with the human tibia, and the sea conch . . . compose for the most part, their religious band. Harsh as these instruments individually taken might sound to a musical ear, yet when joined together in unison, with the voices of 2 or 3 hundred boys and men, managed with varying modulation from the lowest and softest cadence to the loudest swell, they produced to my ear an effect extremely grand.[18]

The sympathetic response of Captain Turner was not, however, the typical Western response, such as that manifested when Tibetan dances were performed at the 1900 World's Fair, after which they were labeled "devil dances," and in 1924, when secret Chams were presented for a British audience in London. The London program—put together by a filmmaker and former Everest explorer—took place over the objections of Tibetan rulers, who quite accurately foresaw the repercussions. The newspaper reactions afterward were sensationalist, with attention-grabbing headlines such as "Tom-Tom Ceremonies from the Himalayas" and "Music from Skulls."

Today, Cham is presented to Western audiences to evoke a calm tranquillity or to foster healing of the problems of the greater planet. It also allows monks to fund-raise for their monastery, teach the dharma, and create political

TIBETAN SACRED DANCE

awareness of the occupation of Tibet by the Communist Chinese. His Holiness the Fourteenth Dalai Lama is acutely aware of the dilemma that arises when extremely ritualistic spiritual practices are presented as cultural entertainment. In an address he gave when the Gyuto tantric monks first went to Europe in 1973, he said:

> Before the public performance of these rites, some people may say "Why are they performing publicly what should be esoteric rites?" Perhaps these people feel that secret teachings should not be turned into a theatrical spectacle. But they needn't be concerned. The secret interior path and its processes are things which the ordinary eye cannot perceive. What is seen outside is totally different. Based on their inner achievement, the Yogis can unfold energies which can serve the benefit of the entire country, such as in ceremonies which consecrate images and icons, exorcise negative forces, prevent natural disasters and epidemics, and uplift the spirit of the times. Thus, from a certain point of view, these ceremonies have a great benefit for the whole society, though there is a valid point in reserving certain ceremonies from public performance. [19]

He also discussed the difference between what the audience might see and what the performers or practitioners experience:

> Although it is not possible to witness the interior processes that are the substantial realities underlying these rites, or the clairvoyant visions that occur during the subsequent contemplative practices, one can observe the exterior aspects of the rites associated with the inner practices, aspects such as those of the Mandalas. We feel there is a beneficial result from seeing these creations, since they create a subconscious affinity with the practices and they purify one's instincts.[20]

This is in line with what Tibetan dance masters say as well. Within Tibetan philosophic studies, dance falls under the four karmas of pacifying, magnetizing, enriching, and destroying. Dance is one of the categories of practices that enrich, increasing merit and prolonging life. The dances are said to eliminate the eighty-four thousand mental afflictions, the most prominent of which are attachment, pride, and ignorance, and transform them into their opposites—spaciousness, equanimity, and mirrorlike wisdom.

2 ACHI LHAMO:
Folk Dance and Operatic Traditions

*The Lhamo in its original and simple way reveals the true,
inherent qualities of the Tibetan: his rough individualism
concealed by an easygoing nature; his deep reverence yet sly
understanding of archaic institutions; his ability to fall and laugh
at pain, sorrow, and death; and moreover his earnest if not always
successful desire to live up to the precepts of Buddhism.*

—Jamyang Norbu, former director of the
Tibetan Institute of Performing Arts

*Actors and dancers should have bodies that are charming and
move beautifully. They should understand how to portray heroism,
ugliness, or humor as well as laughter. They should know how to
swear, hurl insults, show fear, display sympathy and calm.*

A *NGOMPA* OR BLUE
MASK (FISH HUNTER)

—Traditional

In elaborate and colorful costumes, heroes and heroines, villains, mythical creatures, and magicians take the stage to portray the story of Prince Norsang in song and dance. A small kingdom in southern India has been divided into two. In the southern part—under the rule of an evil king who has abandoned Buddhism and surrounded himself with demons and devils—drought and disease have come to prevail. The *nagas* (water spirits) from the south have taken refuge in the peaceful north, where the king practices the Buddha dharma. The southern king can regain peace and prosperity for his kingdom only if the nagas return, so he sends his evil magician after them. When a fisherman tries to save the nagas, an intricate story unfolds, with heroic deeds, evil machinations, love, jealousy, and the ultimate triumph of good over evil. *Prince Norsang*—the first formal Achi Lhamo opera—was adapted from the Indian *Jatakas,* folktales of the previous lives of the Buddha. It was written in the eighteenth century by Rinchen Tsering Wangdu and premiered during the reign of the Seventh Dalai Lama.

Like all Achi Lhamo, *Prince Norsang* is an entertaining presentation that imparts an important religious story. Although both Cham and Achi Lhamo reflect the Buddhist culture of Tibet, the folk tradition of Achi Lhamo dance and opera has an entirely different purpose from the powerful purification and ritual aspects of sacred monastic Cham dance. The performers do not experience any kind of religious or meditative transformation; in fact, Lhamo actors were originally considered to be a bit disreputable. And a most important difference compared with Cham is that many of the performers of Achi Lhamo dance are women.

Achi Lhamo resembles any fine theatrical performance. The costumes, makeup, masks, songs, and dances are designed to capture the hearts and imaginations of the audience, and the scenery and staging enhance the telling of the tale. All aspects of the actors' performances—movement, lyrics, and music—blend together to develop the plot. The operas present real people's problems as well as mythical accomplishments and cultural history, along with an abundance of humor and political innuendo. These performances are not for children, although their embodiment of what is referred to as the mythic imagination stands in contradistinction to the social, critical tradition of most Western theater.

MASKED DANCERS
FROM HEMIS
MONASTERY

ORIGINS AND DEVELOPMENT OF ACHI LHAMO

EARLY ORIGINS

Tibetan opera—one of the oldest continuous living theaters in the world—has long and distinguished roots. The first performances of Lhamo were probably composed of songs and teachings of the Buddha, with a heritage that can be traced back to plays known as the *Birth Stories of the Buddha* written in the first century C.E. by Ashvaghosha of India. In addition to composing well-known poems in honor of the Buddha, Ashvaghosha wrote many plays on his

life, adhering to the rules of drama put forth by Bharata in his *Natyashastra (Study of Dramatic Arts),* reflecting Indian performance traditions whose origins are estimated to date from 4000 B.C.E.

The operas also have touches of Chinese, Mongolian, and Nepalese traditions weaving through them. It is not even too far-fetched to say that they display a smattering of Greek influence, spread by trading route contacts during the time of Alexander the Great.

THANGTONG
GYALPO, BUILDER
OF IRON BRIDGES
IN THE
HIMALAYAS AND
FOUNDER OF
ACHI LHAMO

THANGTONG GYALPO

Although differing accounts exist about the origins of Achi Lhamo, the founding of the more formal operatic tradition is popularly attributed to Thangtong Gyalpo, a fourteenth-century engineer and builder of bridges who helped to connect the people of Tibet and advance the spread of Buddhist culture throughout the countryside. His name, given to him by the dakinis, means "King of the Empty Plains," referring to his journeys to India, China, Mongolia, Bhutan, Kashmir, and Ladakh. It is said that he uttered the well-known mantra *Om Mani Padme Hum* at the moment of his birth, and he is as highly regarded in Tibet as Leonardo da Vinci is in the West.

Although many legends are associated with him, his existence as a real, historical person is substantiated both by the Fifth Dalai Lama, who authenticated his *Gsan Yig* text, and by the work of the nineteenth-century scholars Jamgon Khyentse Rinpoche and Jamgon Kongtrul Lodro Thaye, who collected many of his teachings for his *namthar,* or religious biography. He is revered for his teachings on the life of Avalokiteshvara, the deity of compassion. Thangtong taught the mantra and meditations connected with Avalokiteshvara to the wild nomads of Kong-po, shepherds from his home village in eastern Tibet. In fact, it was his desire to help all sentient beings, coupled with his own visions, that led him to become a great bridge builder.

The story attributing the origins of Achi Lhamo to Thangtong Gyalpo is connected to a journey he made to Kong-po to raise funds for building bridges. With the support of several wealthy friends who supplied him with essential tools as well as access to an iron mine, he built his first iron-linked bridge near Chushur. However, in an unfortunate accident, all of the iron links he forged for the bridge fell into the river. One version of the story says that seven brothers (Poon-doon) in a nearby village were willing to help him start all over again since a bridge would greatly benefit the surrounding area. But Thangtong Gyalpo had no more money. In order to raise the necessary cash, he organized the brothers into a wandering minstrel troupe of the kind that was, no doubt, already in existence. The dancers must have been really good because villagers were said to remark, "The gods themselves are dancing." This version is supported by the fact that until China invaded Tibet, there was a troupe called The Seven Brothers of Chongye who claimed to have a direct lineage connection with the original troupe of Lhamo dancers.

The only problem with this explanation is that *lhamo* is a term for a goddess and *achi* means "sister." Another version of the story says that seven sisters well versed in music and dance set off to various provinces of central Tibet to raise money for the bridge, taking responsibility for "the beating of the drum and the clash of the cymbal." The catalog of the Tibetan Institute of Performing Arts says that Thangtong Gyalpo trained seven sisters from his crew to sing and dance while he accompanied them on the drums. "Onlookers, struck by their beauty, exclaimed, 'the Lhamo (goddesses) themselves are dancing,' which gave rise to the name Lhamo."[1] Tashi Dhundup, one of the founders of Chaksampa, a Lhamo dance troupe, says Thangtong Gyalpo "had a vision, a dream of Tara, who gave him seven chains and those chains transformed into these dancers."[2]

Yet another version says Thangtong Gyalpo built the bridge but jealous spirits came and destroyed it at night. Distraught, he prayed for help to his personal protective deity, the goddess Tara, the embodiment of the female energy of compassionate action. Tara appeared to him as an old woman—one of her common guises—and gave him seven magical chain links. When he encountered the jealous spirit, he threw the chain links to the ground. They magically transformed into seven auspicious dancers who hypnotized the spirit, allowing Thangtong to capture it with a spell and go on to rebuild the bridge.

A final version says Thangtong subdued a demon who was locked in stone. The demon then emanated six other versions of himself as a crazy man and all seven of them (including the original) went to the marketplace and performed a dance to raise the money to build the bridge.

TSERING WANGMO PERFORMING IN NEW YORK CITY

Although each of these popular stories honors Thangtong Gyalpo as the creator of Achi Lhamo, this fact is not mentioned in his biography, *Gyurme Dechen Norbu Melong*. Dance, music, and plays were certainly well known in India and Tibet before his time; a copy of one of Ashvaghosha's first-century plays—a dramatic rendering of the life of the Buddha—was found sealed up in the walls of a central Asian Silk Route monastery located at Turfan, an area once ruled by Tibet. Also, a type of refined folk dance—a court dance called Gar—was performed for the royalty at Lhasa in earlier centuries. However, it is very possible that Thangtong Gyalpo did form a song-and-dance troupe to raise money for bridge building and that they became so good at performing that they became a tradition.

In any case, all Tibetans revere Thangtong Gyalpo, and he is credited with building fifty-eight iron suspension bridges, sixty wooden bridges, and 118 ferries in Tibet. Boatmen pray to him when a river rises or becomes dangerous. A common tradition was to build *chortens* (stupas) to him in spots that were known to flood. At the Norbulingka, the summer palace of the Dalai Lamas—prone to summer flooding from the Kyichu River—thousands of his images were built inside the walls. When anyone moves, a statue of Thangtong Gyalpo—or, if one is not available, a mortar and pestle representing him—is first placed in the new home. Construction workers place small statues of him in the walls of new buildings. Even physicians have a place for him in their lineage trees.

PRINCE NORSANG
WITH HIS ATTENDANTS

⊡ An Arrow Points to the Future ⊡

While still a boy, Thangtong Gyalpo entered the Kagyu Monastery of Chang Ting, spending a long time in meditative retreat, including one seven-year retreat after his mother died. He later became a well-known *chod*—cemetery grounds—practitioner, meditating upon the impermanent and illusory nature of worldly existence.

One day, as he walked on the bank of the Kyichu River, he saw a man carrying a bow and arrow. Thangtong asked if he could try it out and the man let him shoot some arrows. When he was finished, he thanked the man and kept walking.

When he passed by the river much later and saw one of the arrows that he had shot floating downstream, he took it as a sign that he should build bridges and ferries to connect Tibet for the benefit of all sentient beings. In those times this was a saintly task, for high mountains, deep gorges, and treacherous passes could suddenly collapse during the spring melting of snowy mountains, making traveling a life-and-death experience. To this day, Thangtong Gyalpo is a revered hero and is considered a saint by many Tibetans.

STATUE OF THANGTONG GYALPO

A MAN OF "WILD THEATRE" WITH HIS TRUMPET OF HUMAN THIGHBONE

DEVELOPMENT OF ACHI LHAMO

Originally Achi Lhamo was performed in public squares and could go on for days. The stage had few props, so the audience would fill in the blanks with their imagination. The actors used simple makeup and masks with distinct characterizations, enabling the characters to be easily identified as good or bad, loyal or duplicitous. Early performances were probably pantomime with an emphasis on dancing; literary content was added later on. Over time, the operas evolved from comparatively simple presentations to much more elaborate and theatrical extravaganzas. As Lhamo became more codified, different individuals and government offices would sponsor the troupes, often loaning them clothes and masks, so the performers started wearing the most aristocratic brocades and silks from Russia and China. Their accessories were inlaid with jewels from India, China, and Europe.

TIBETAN FAMILY OF MUSICIANS AND ACTORS. PHOTO BY SIR CHARLES BELL, 1933–34

Achi Lhamo first became well documented during the reign of the Fifth Dalai Lama in the seventeenth century, its popularity attested to by murals and records from that time. As the themes and stories of the operas were passed down through the generations, people knew them so well that any variation in content or context was noted instantly. By the end of the nineteenth century, every major Tibetan district had a Lhamo troupe and ever since then it has been an elaborate part of both religious and cultural festivals.

MAJOR OPERAS

OPPOSITE: CONFLICT
BETWEEN GOOD AND
EVIL. THE CHARACTER
KNEELING IS BEGGING
FOR HIS LIFE.

The operas are presented in specific sequences and are thematically centered on either important religious events of Tibet or stories that migrated from India and were adapted. Most stories comprise a simple plot depicting a conflict between good and bad or being religious or nonreligious. A wicked

demon, queen, or minister may show up in contrast to a saintly prince or princess, who usually suffers some kind of torture or cruelty at their hands until an eventual return to triumph. There are many major operas—including *Prince Norsang, Drowa Sangmo, Gyalsa Bhelsa, King Gesar of Ling, Pema Woebar, Rechung's Travels to Central Tibet with Milarepa, Sukyi Nyima, Thepa Tenpa, Nangsa Woebum, Chungpo Dhonyoe Dhondup, Durke Kundai, Tin gyi Zhopa,* and *Jhowo Je Palden Atisha*—several of which are summarized below.

DROWA SANGMO

Drowa Sangmo tells the story of the reign of King Kala Wangpo of Mon, in the present-day northeast of India. After witnessing his wife and children suffer through extremely difficult times, he becomes a Buddhist practitioner and encourages the rest of the people in his country to become practitioners as well.

Drowa Sangmo is one of the most-beloved Tibetan operas because it includes many references to early Tibetan folklore, history, and the introduction of Buddhism.

JOKERS OR *ATSARAS* IMITATING MINISTERS, INDIA

GYALSA BHELSA

This story relates to the reign of King Songtsen Gampo in the eighth century. When the king expands his kingdom to upper Burma and western China, he wishes to form marriage alliances with princesses of both Nepal and China. As part of their dowries, he asks for their country's most sacred images of the Buddha—the Jho Mingyur Dorjee of Nepal and the Jowo Shakyamuni Buddha of China. The Nepalese are delighted and send their daughter Tritsun along with the sacred image. But when Gampo sends his minister Gar Tongtsen to China, the emperor asks him to perform a number of difficult and tricky tasks to get the princess for his king. The Chinese emperor is so impressed with Gar Tongtsen's accomplishments that he sends Princess Wen Cheng off to Tibet with the holy image, accompanied by another Tibetan minister, but demands that Gar remain with him. Having

OPPOSITE: A JOKER
AMUSING THE CROWD

ACTORS PERFORMING
LHAMO FOLK
DANCING

125

TIBETAN SACRED DANCE

told the princess and her escort to wait for him at the border, Gar uses a feigned illness and a series of tricks to escape from the court and join the princess, taking her back to Tibet, where the overjoyed officials perform the *gyal gzhas,* or royal dance.

KING GESAR OF LING

Originating in Kham, the eastern nomadic area of Tibet, *King Gesar of Ling* is Tibet's epic warrior story, as important and intricate as the West's Homeric epics. Starting as part of oral folk traditions and passed down through the generations for almost a thousand years, it is still sung today in Tibet and is known in different areas along the Silk Route, particularly China. The longest epic known to the world, it has 120-odd volumes, with more than a million verses, totaling over twenty million words, in which long prose sections alternate with hundreds of epic ballads.

King Gesar of Ling tells the story of a enlightened warrior named Gesar who battles against evil, yet his ultimate battle—like that for most of us—is with his inner demons. Though his story is a blend of legend and reality, he is believed to have been a real king who ruled Ling in eastern Tibet around 1050 C.E. At

THE STATE ORACLE AND HIS SECRETARY. THE STATE ORACLE WIELDS HIS SWORD WHILE HIS SECRETARY RECORDS THE PROPHECIES.

ACTOR BEING MADE UP AS KING GESAR. PHOTO BY ANNA FUENTES

the beginning of the epic he is a Buddhist deity named Good News, living peaceably in a Buddhist heaven. In the first volume of the epic—the *Lha gLing,* or *The Divine Land of Ling*—the Tibetan tantric Padmasambhava and the bodhisattva of compassion, Avalokiteshvara, try to get him mixed up in worldly affairs.

Gesar is incarnated into this world as the son of a god and a naga princess to subdue the demon kings in the areas surrounding Ling. To do this he asks for the assistance of his friends, wife, and horse—who are also incarnated deities with magical powers. His epic abounds with descriptions of his miraculous feats that include numerous physical transformations and phantom appearances. Conquering the neighboring lands with magic and arms, he converts the local tribes to Buddhism. Gesar's version of Buddhism accepts the world as it is and transforms it by working with local and universal energies, rather than retreating into strict asceticism.

In Tibet his story was told by songs known as *Drung,* recited from memory by traveling male and female bards called *Drungpas* and *Drungmas* who recalled the events vividly from what they described as their past lives when they were actually subjects of the kingdom of Ling. That tradition seems to have been almost wiped out by the Communist Chinese. Still, his dances are presented in monasteries in Lhasa and throughout the country, as well as in the Dzogchen Monastery in south India. The forms and props for chanting and telling the Gesar story vary by region.

ANIMAL CHARACTERS
FROM A LHAMO
PERFORMANCE

PEMA WOEBAR

In an Indian kingdom of Mutik Sheer there was an evil king, Lonpey Chojey, his cunning minister, Swiftfoot, and an intelligent merchant called Norsang. The king—jealous of Norsang's fame and power—sends him on a journey to get the wish-fulfilling gem from the queen of the nagas. Although Norsang does not want to go, he is forced to. On the way, his boat is attacked by giant scorpions and he dies. After six months Padmasambhava sees Norsang's lovely wife Lharing Dhamsey in mourning. He sends light rays into her body and she gives birth to a son, Pema Woebar, the "Lotus of Blazing Light."

OPPOSITE: THE EVIL KING, LONPEY CHOJEY

GIANT SCORPIONS PREPARING TO ATTACK NORSANG

Pema is precocious and wonders about his father, but his mother tells him nothing. He steals wool from her and spins eighteen luminous threads that he takes to the market. An old woman then buys them and tells him about his father. The king—who is watching through a telescope from his palace—sees the luminous threads and sends Swiftfoot to investigate. Swiftfoot threatens to kill the old woman if she does not say where the threads came from. She relents, and the king orders Swiftfoot to find Pema Woebar, which he does by threatening the life of Lharing Dhamsey.

The king meets Pema Woebar and says he will adopt him, but first he must go to the sea and get the wish-fulfilling gem of the queen of the nagas. The dakinis give Pema a mantra to protect him from all obstacles and he

SNOW LION DANCE,
NEW YORK CITY,
1991

brings back the gem to his mother. The king—angry that the gem was not delivered to him—orders Pema to get the magic pan that carries people across the skies. Pema overcomes obstacles to get the magic pan, in which he is accompanied back to the king's court by five dakinis. After the dakinis leave, the king tells Pema he will be executed for having more wives than he does. After the executioners fail in their attempts to set his pyre on fire, Pema compassionately allows them to kill him so they will not be killed. The dakinis gather his ashes and transfer his consciousness to another body, then go to the court and announce Pema's death. They take the king and Swiftfoot for a ride in the magic pan, which descends to the land of the demons, where the king and Swiftfoot are eaten. Then Pema is reborn from a lotus flower in the form of Padmasambhava.

MAGICAL PARROT PROPHESYING TO IGNORANT HUMANS. FROM A PERFORMANCE OF THE OPERA *SUKYI NYIMA*

RECHUNG U PHEB (RECHUNG'S TRAVELS TO CENTRAL TIBET WITH MILAREPA)

This is the story of the famous yogi Milarepa and his disciple Rechung. In his youth Milarepa practiced black magic to take revenge on relatives who deprived his mother of the family inheritance. He later realizes how degraded his behavior was and seeks Buddhist teachings. After undergoing arduous tests

ABOVE AND LEFT:
LOBSANG
SAMTEN
TEACHING CHAM
STEPS IN NEW
YORK CITY

OPPOSITE:
ATSARAS MAKING
MUSIC, INDIA

and ordeals under his teacher Marpa, a lay master, he receives initiation from him. He then spends the rest of his life meditating and teaching his disciples through the composition of one hundred thousand songs, or *dohas*. Rechung—one of his chief disciples—recorded Milarepa's life story as they traveled and meditated in remote mountain caves. The Tibetan Institute of Performing Arts (TIPA) produced a new version of this opera in honor of the year 2000, written by the Venerable Lobsang Samten.

SUKYI NYIMA

In a kingdom of India, an old couple seeking teachings from the saintly old hermit Dhangsong present him with a white loincloth. That night he has a wet dream while wearing the loincloth. The next morning he washes the cloth at a stream and a doe comes to drink water at the shore. She becomes preg-

nant and gives birth to a human girl whom Dhansong cares for and names Sukyi Nyima (Sun's Body). Sukyi Nyima contentedly grows up with Dhansong in his cave.

The old king of the land names his eldest son Dawa Senge (Moon's Lion) as his successor and tells him to visit the state temple to ask for a prophecy. When Dawa Senge asks the oracle where he will find his wife, he is told she will come from the south. Knowing this, a low-caste girl, Rigngen Bhumo, disguises herself as a princess and serves the new king *chang* (beer). He becomes infatuated with her and marries her, ignoring the warning of a magical parrot.

When a boar starts damaging the palace garden, Rigngen Bhumo tells a hunter to kill it. The hunter follows the boar and discovers Sukyi Nyima, then returns to the palace and tells King Dawa Senge of his discovery. The king meets Sukyi Nyima and falls in love, begging her to marry him. Dhansong, the hermit, gives his daughter a *mala* (rosary) of 108 pearls with magical properties to protect her.

RIGNGEN BHUMO, DISGUISED AS A PRINCESS, SERVING THE NEW KING *CHANG* (BEER). FROM THE OPERA *SUKYI NYIMA*

DAKINIS CELEBRATING
THE BIRTH OF SUKYI
NYIMA'S SON

After Sukyi Nyima marries the king, Rigngen Bhumo arranges for her to be served by Yama, an evil maid. Yama tries to put a curse on her mistress, but it does not work. To find out why, Yama goes to an astrologer and learns all about Sukyi Nyima's magical beads. After replacing them with fake ones, she is able to make Sukyi Nyima sick with her curse.

Yama and the evil queen Rigngen Bhumo conspire to make the king believe Sukyi Nyima is evil. They first kill a white elephant, and then Sukyi Nyima's own son, making it appear that she is responsible. The king becomes angry when he finds the dead white elephant and his dead son and wants to kill Sukyi Nyima. The parrot tells the king he is wrong. The king kills the parrot, whose blood is white, proving Sukyi Nyima's innocence. But Sukyi Nyima is taken away to the cremation grounds to be eaten by animals. Her deer mother shows up and sets her free with the help of the other animals.

Sukyi Nyima goes to a cave to meditate and becomes a nun. Yama comes to her to confess her sins and gives her back her authentic pearl mala. After one of the king's ministers hears Sukyi Nyima preach and tells him about it,

the king visits the nun and recognizes her. He apologizes for his bad actions. She returns to the palace and the king punishes Rigngen Bhumo and Yama. Sukyi Nyima has another son named Nyime Senge (Sun's Lion). Everyone celebrates and Buddhism is spread throughout the land.

THEPA TENPA

This opera was written by Nya Khampa, a monk from Lhasa, after the Thirteenth Dalai Lama fled Lhasa in 1904. First performed in 1909, it is a unique piece using only solo singers, without a full operatic chorus. The libretto is recited in a manner reminiscent of chanting. The introduction of the characters comes through music, and it proceeds in a more leisurely pace than traditional opera.

TRADITIONAL TIBETAN WOMAN'S COSTUME

CHUNGPO DHONYOE DHONDUP

This is a story of two half brothers—Dhondup and Dhonyo—born to King Topkyvilha. After Dhondup is born to the king's wife, Princess Kunsangma, the princess dies from illness and the king remarries. His new wife, Pemachen, gives birth to Dhonyo. The half brothers become inseparable. But because Pemachen wants her son to succeed to the throne, she poisons the king's mind by saying that Dhondup is the reincarnation of a demon. When Dhondup is banished to the forest, his loyal brother Dhonyo follows him. Through various twists in the story, Dhondup thinks Dhonyo is dead, but he is not. Dhondup meets the beautiful daughter of the king of Yu Ling and marries her, but not before he is almost executed for being a demon. Eventually, he finds his half brother Dhonyo, and they return to their father's house in time for Dhonyo to inherit King Topkyvilha's kingdom. Dhondup, in turn, becomes king of Yu Ling and, as in all fairy tales, they live happily ever after.

Actor
lamenting,
India

NANGSA WOEBUM (OBUM)

This is a story that originates from a local legend in central Tibet about a young girl who devotes her life to the dharma. An elderly couple who are devoted Buddhists live in a remote Tibetan village. Though they are both quite old, one night the wife has a vision of the goddess Tara in her sleep and nine months later she gives birth to a daughter named Nangsa. She grows into a beautiful maiden with many suitors but wishes to become a nun. One day she goes to a religious festival, where she is spied by an aristocrat from Rinag who demands that she marry his son. Although she tells him she is not fit to be a nobleman's wife, he persists and places a turquoise on her head, declaring that he will kill any man who dares to marry her. The next day the nobleman appears at her parents' doorstep, saying he has come to make the dowry payment. Nangsa cries out that she would rather meditate until she dies than marry. But when her parents warn her that the lord might kill all of them if she refuses, she agrees to marry him.

After a year Nangsa bears a son. Her life at her husband's palace is one of misery. Her sister-in-law, a spinster, never gives Nangsa the keys to the household storeroom and generally makes her life hell. One day while Nangsa is in

Man portraying
pregnant
woman

the fields harvesting barley, two pilgrims pass by and she offers them grain from the fields, not the storeroom. Still, her sister-in-law hits her for her generosity and complains bitterly to her brother, Nangsa's husband, who then beats his wife, breaking three of her ribs. Shortly afterward another pilgrim (her future teacher) passes by the palace, singing a parable about suffering and a beautiful woman. Deeply moved, Nangsa gives him the jewels she wears around her neck. Her husband—who has been listening at the door—enters in a rage. The beggar leaps out of the window but Nangsa's husband beats her so violently he inadvertently murders her. An astrologer warns him not to burn her body because she will return from the dead in seven days, which she does, vowing celibacy.

When her in-laws and husband plead with her not to abandon them, she relents, but when she visits her parents, she confides that she still wants to be a nun. This vexes her mother, who tells her how stupid she is to ignore her husband and his beautiful palace and long for celibacy. Nangsa runs to the mountains to find her lama and ask him for teachings. When he says that she is not yet ready, she pulls a knife out from under her skirt and threatens to kill herself. He relents and gives her tantric initiation. But Nangsa's husband pursues her with an army, which kills many meditators and captures her. The soldiers even capture her teacher and insult him by saying:

> You are an old dog that has seduced our snow lion!
> Why did you try to rape this white grouse?
> Why did you pull out her feathers and wings?
> You are an old donkey living in a dirty stable.
> Why did you rape our beautiful wild horse?
> You nasty old bull, why did you have sex
> With our beautiful white female yak?

The master then moves the surrounding mountains and brings the dead disciples back to life. Nangsa levitates and mocks the soldiers' attempts to control her. When the soldiers see her flying over them, they drop their weapons and became practitioners, as do her abusive husband and vindictive sister-in-law.

Early Western Encounters with Achi Lhamo

RUTH ST. DENIS AND GENERAL LADEN-LA,
WITH CHAM DANCERS, DARJEELING, 1926.
FROM THE PERSONAL PHOTO ALBUMS OF RUTH
ST. DENIS AND TED SHAWN, NEW YORK CITY
PUBLIC LIBRARY, LINCOLN CENTER

Travel diaries were often the only information available to the newly industrialized world back home about distant and exotic countries. In the mid-1800s two extremely fortunate French-speaking priests—Evariste Régis Huc and Joseph Gabet—found themselves in Lhasa during the New Year's festival and recorded in their travel journal their impressions of what was probably a performance of either acrobats or Achi Lhamo:

"On the principle square, and in front of the public monuments, you see from morning until night, troupes of comedians and tumblers amusing the people with their representation . . . now singing, now dancing and exhibiting feats of strength and agility. . . . Their dress consists of a cap, surmounted by long pheasant plumes, a black mask adorned with a white beard of prodigious length, large white pantaloons and a green tunic coming down to the knees and bound round the waist by a yellow girdle."[3]

Hamilton Boner's diary of his journey across Tibet, published in 1894, tells of a hilarious encounter with a wandering troupe of performers, one of the many bands that roamed the Tibetan countryside: "A troupe of professional dancers gave us a performance. The first part was much the same as the masked dance at Hemis (Monastery) but without the masks. They began by walking round in slow time, striking a drum and chanting a mournful dirge. Then the time quickened and round and round they whirled in true dancing dervish style until they had to stop for want of breath. They then danced a variety of the same figure in which one of them had two swords in each hand and turned somersaults. . . . One of them had a five-stringed banjo, on which he played a tune with remarkably few notes in it. After they had been rewarded and had departed another troupe, consisting of two men and a boy sat down with much solemnity, disclosing to view an umbrella-like arrangement decorated with bright beads and lumps of bone. This was slowly turned round while a terribly mournful sound—tune I cannot call it, was given forth by the company. They were hastily rewarded and requested to move on. The reward was purposely fixed on a low scale to discourage others, but still it must have been too high, as no sooner had they gone than an ugly old woman took their place, disclosed similar paraphernalia, and began in the most unmusical voice I have ever heard, to chant a dirge appalling in its mournfulness. She also was hastily induced to move on, and as her song ceased, we felt a relief like the sudden cessation of pain."[4]

ESSENTIAL ELEMENTS OF ACHI LHAMO

PHASES OF ACHI LHAMO PERFORMANCE

Every performance starts with the purification of the stage, *don* or *r ngon-pa-dan,* by three or seven individuals referred to as "fish hunters" or "blue masks" *(ngompas).* The *ngompas* sometimes sing a long chant that begins like this:

TASHI DHUNDUP OF
CHAKSAMPA SPINNING
TO PURIFY THE STAGE

Standing in this crystal village
That lies behind the hills
Oh juniper, tree of gods,
It is said your sweet scent
Pervades the realm of gods above.

Next come the earth purification rituals, including the "Taming of the Earth" ritual and the "Auspicious Rites" ritual. "White masks," or *gyalus*—two rather stationary figures who wear long flowing robes—usually appear in the opening as well.

Then women come onstage to join the chorus; they take turns playing assorted goddesses and sing a four-part song called "Ascent of the Auspicious Staircase." One woman begins by singing:

> Ema Mani Padme Hum
> Ema Mani Padme Hum.

The second girl adds:

> Look up at that mountain
> The mists circling it to the right.
> The great meditator
> Lives on the mountain.
> Look up at him who has great realizations.

And the third:

> May my guru know,
> May the one of the Iron Bridge know.
> Respectful prostrations
> To the feet of Thangtong Gyalpo.

And the fourth sings:

> There is never any addition or subtraction
> In the sayings of the peerless Buddhas.
> May the obstacles of the Enchanting Ones
> Who are like the White Lotus
> Be cleared.

Ngompa
SPINNING

After the stage is purified, the main narrator appears. He gives a stylized rendition of the opera, ending with a shout. Later he reappears to explain each scene, often announcing the entrances and exits of the main characters, who appear from the wings. These characters usually enter dancing, accompanied by two musicians who sit down on the edge of the stage to play, usually on a lute, two-stringed fiddle, hammer dulcimer, or flute. If the performance is short, the narrator might read the dialogue that is usually sung.

LHAMO MUSICIANS
PLAYING DULCIMER
AND TWO-STRINGED
FIDDLE

The main body of the opera *(gzhung)* comes next, in which the story is told with song and dance. The performance ends with an epilogue *(bkra-shis)* and a blessing. Finally, a special song and dance is done to request the audience to donate money.

TYPES OF PERFORMERS

The main characters of the dramas include various kings and queens, princes and princesses, hermits, demons, evil plotters, common folk, and magical beings. Although Achi Lhamo and Cham portray many of the same characters—such as Padmasambhava, King Songtsen Gampo and his wives, and Milarepa—they have very different meanings in the two traditions. In Lhamo, the characters are used to dramatize a moral story about good triumphing over evil, while in Cham they represent mythic and transcendent elements.

Achi Lhamo operas also feature several other types of actors who are responsible for specific tasks.

The purification of the stage is taken care of by the ngompas, who wear large masks with beards and baggy pants tucked into black boots. While turning cartwheels, they swirl the tasseled ropes wrapped around their waists to create a wheel-like effect.

Tradition holds that the gyalus—whose name refers to the oldest man in a family—are included at the start of a performance because the old men in the audiences of the performances given by Thangtong Gyalpo's group were so moved they joined in the joking, singing, and dancing. These dancers carry a cane and wear large round yellow hats and knee-length woolen shirts (chuba) with intricate collars. In certain texts gyalus are referred to as princes.

The women who sing in the chorus also play assorted goddesses called Khandro Riknga (Dakinis of the Five Families).

The main narrator, wearing a fancy chuba and beautiful boots, presents the story and the main characters.

The Tashi Chopa—an auspicious old man who symbolizes long life and good fortune—appears at either the beginning or the end of a Lhamo performance. He wears a mask trimmed with white goat hair to look like the face of a bearded elderly man and holds an arrow braided in four different colors of silk to call down the energy of wealth.

SINGING

The stories are sung by the main characters in a rapid chanting style called *namthar* (arias), not to be confused with sacred biographies, also called *namthar*. Almost all characters involved in the production sing in the chorus, repeating or summarizing the refrain of each stanza sung by the lead singer. The basic poetic structure of the songs is lines six or eight syllables long in two- or four-line stanzas. The stanzas are combined with nonsense syllables that introduce the tune of the score and keep the melody going on past the time when the song has finished. The performers often make up verses as well, especially during humorous scenes, with sly references to contemporary events, thus making each performance unique.

A TRAINEE AT THE TIBETAN INSTITUTE OF PERFORMING ARTS PRACTICES HER SINGING.

TIBETAN SACRED DANCE

At least twenty different song melodies are used to portray different moods, such as:

Gdang-ring, for joy, ease of mind
Skyo-glu, for sorrow, grief
Gdang-thung, for narration in general
Gdang-log, for emotional change

The operas use specific songs to accompany various events like drinking beer, courting a girl, constructing a house, begging, playing dice games, making up the accounts, snide political criticism, and even getting ready to go into battle. There are educated court songs *(glu),* spring songs *(glin glu),* and special songs for weddings, including songs to accompany the spinning of complex riddles such as "What are thirty-two mountains glowing?" Special songs

signify the stages of farming such as plowing the fields, harvesting the grain, and threshing the plants. One song about fieldwork says,

> Paring, combing, sort it out with the wind.
> The work is easy.

In the past, folksingers spent most of their lives traveling and their status was very low, like that of beggars, even though they lived by chanting. Roving bands traveled throughout the countryside singing epic songs, offering not only entertainment, but also spiritual and moral instruction. Songs like the street songs of Lhasa also were used to openly and politically criticize the government. The street songs were then usually picked up and sung by women at the village gossip locales and while doing the laundry. Perhaps this was the reason that—at least in medieval Tibet—the government regarded actors and musicians as tawdry and disreputable necessities.

But the aristocracy also wrote songs, as did the Fifth Dalai Lama, who wrote:

> East, from the mountain's peak
> The clear white moon has appeared.
> A young girl's countenance
> Comes to form in my mind.
> Last year fresh grass was planted
> Now heaps of bundled straw;
> Young, growing old male bodies
> Are stiffer than southern war bows.

Most songs were written anonymously. The writer would put down the lyrics on pieces of paper and scatter them about the road around a monastery. If the song was found, pieced together, and well received by pilgrims and caravanners, it would spread throughout the land. In the early twentieth century, modified versions of folk songs and dances from western and central Tibet—

called *stod gzhas,* or "western songs"—became popular in Lhasa. From more recent times, here is an example of a street song after the invasion of the Communist army in the 1950s:

> This liberation army has arrived,
> The herd of beggars has arrived.
> Everyone has been liberated,
> Everyone has been made beggars.

Lhamo singing uses a specific technique of throat vibration called *dingu* or *mgrin-khug.* Since performances were originally done in the open air, the actors needed to have powerful voices that could be projected over a long distance. A common technique used to strengthen the voice was to practice under the roar of a waterfall. Learning to project against the thunderous sound of tons of falling water built up lung strength and stamina. This technique is still practiced by members of the Tibetan Institute of Performing Arts in India.

MEMBERS OF THE TIBETAN INSTITUTE OF PERFORMING ARTS (TIPA) REHEARSE SINGING OUTDOORS.

MUSIC REHEARSAL AT TIPA

OPPPOSITE: TIPA LHAMO PERFORMER PRACTICING VOICE PROJECTION AT BAGSUNATH FALLS, DHARAMSALA, INDIA

MUSIC AND INSTRUMENTS

The music played in Achi Lhamo performances is *nangma,* the "chamber music" of Tibet. It uses a heterophonic (seven-note) style where every instrument ornaments the same melodic theme in a unique way. The rhythmic elements in nangma are those most common in Tibet, and even the dancers' feet

TIPA MEMBERS
PRACTICING LONG
HORNS *(RADONGS)*

use the rhythm in fast dances. The beats are most commonly divided into a short/long sub rhythm and can also be found in ritual chants. Within a song there might be a fast dance called a *shabdro* or a slow section called *te-she*. The most famous nangma is called *Amaleho,* one of about sixty songs attributed to the Sixth Dalai Lama.

PLAYING *RADONGS* IN
PERFORMANCE

STRINGED LUTE
(*TCHA-NIEN*)

WOMAN PLAYING
DULCIMER, NEW
YORK CITY

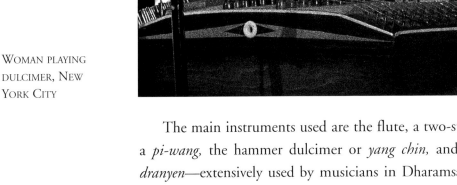

The main instruments used are the flute, a two-stringed fiddle known as a *pi-wang,* the hammer dulcimer or *yang chin,* and a long-necked lute or *dranyen*—extensively used by musicians in Dharamsala—that comes in two sizes, with the smaller one sounding an octave above the larger one. The wind instruments include conches used only for modulated calls, short trumpets in bone or metal, and long, telescopic trumpets. When Lhamo dancers perform in Lhasa they use a stick to play a central beat, which is varied with a middle type of beat and a beat on the drum edge. Other beat variations include pushing upward, pushing downward, and pushing across beats, using the big thumb, the little finger, and the middle finger. There are even four different styles of clashing cymbals—the full clash, the half clash, forcible, and clashing the edges. Instruments such as the flute and fiddle originally came from southeast Asia and many Tibetans use Chinese instruments.

It is written that Tibetans adopted the pentatonic scale after King Songtsen Gampo brought musicians from China into Tibet in 700 C.E. But before his time Tibetan musicians were important members of the courts of nomadic kings, where many government records were memorized in song form by government workers. Some of the musicians in the early Lhamo troupes were Tibetan Muslims *(kha che),* another source of musical variation. In any case, the word *nangma* comes from the Persian Urdu word *naghma,* meaning "tune" or "melody," and the musical style is shared by many troupes from Morocco, Iraq, Kashmir, Burma, and China.

DULCIMER
(SGRA-SNYAN)

LHAMO PERFORMERS
PLAYING LUTE AND
TWO-STRINGED FIDDLE

Most musical notation focuses on three areas—chanting, drums, and cymbals. Many lines of text have commentaries written in small characters between the lines and connected by dotted lines where there are instructions to "raise" the voice or "lower" it or to play "softly." Drumbeats are represented by a curved stroke.

There is an ongoing controversy between Tibetans who insist that their notation came from India and European scholars who say there is no real notation in Indian music and that the most likely source is either the Nestorian Church in central Asia or the Buddhist monasteries of China and Japan.

Cham and Lhamo musical notation differs in that Cham has a specialized notation and symbolic name for every single instrument and how it is used; in Lhamo, the music depends much more on the movements of the actors.

FOLK DANCE STYLES

The basic styles in Lhamo still conform to the seven parts choreographed by the nineteenth-century master Rigpa for the Kyormolungpa opera troupe, one of the four most prominent Lhamo groups in Tibet:

1. *Don-udar:* slow to quick pace with up-and-down motions, done while entering the stage
2. *Phye-ling:* turning in half circles, first to the right, then to the left, done while marching forward
3. *Phyag-ubul:* salutations, bowing with clasped hands, a gesture with religious connotations
4. *Gar-che:* full circles, moving in a ring, used to indicate embarking on a long journey
5. *Dal-gtong:* slow steps, no music, used mostly at intermission
6. *Uphar-chen:* big circles, spinning with arms extended at an angle of sixty degrees to the ground, related to acrobatics and martial skills
7. *Brel-karb:* rapid dancing

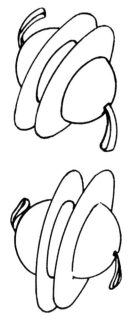

CYMBALS *(SI-NYEC)*

OPPOSITE: A PAIR OF SKELETONS—CITTI PATTI *(TUR TUR TAK BA)*—DANCE TO PURIFY NEGATIVE FORCES. THE SKELETONS SYMBOLIZE IMPERMANENCE.

DANCERS LEAPING IN
UPHAR-CHEM STYLE

The language used to describe the stomping of the feet and accompanying hand gestures is divided by gender. The male style is likened to pulling an apron and the female style is supposed to be like wearing a mala (rosary). Different characters are often identified with their own unique steps, and when a dance step changes significantly it usually means it is the end of a scene.

Different regions also had different dance specialties. The nomadic Khampas of eastern Tibet liked the magnificent *bro* dances with their brisk steps and hearty songs praising the area's panoramic and wild vistas, while the western

Tibetans formed circles and danced energetic *sgor gzhas* characterized by high steps and much cheer and accompanied with a drum and lute. Dancers in Lhasa preferred quick-stepping *stod gzhas,* thought to have originated in the 1920s as adaptations of traditional circle songs. They also performed the *gyal gzhas,* or "royal dance," said to have been originally performed by the aristocracy to welcome the Chinese princess Wen Cheng as the bride of Songtsen Gampo. The common pattern was to start with a series of slow lines, then go to fast lines, speeding up the melody with an enhanced rhythm. Most of these songs are in a five-note (pentatonic) scale with a sixth note added to the conclusion.

ENERGETIC *SGOR GZHAS* DANCE

Besides these popular regional dances, there were many unique ceremonial and district dances. In Kham, wandering dancers known as *ralpas* or *yogis* performed plays in a particularly acrobatic style said to come from the great yogi Milarepa's chief disciple, Rechung. At Sera Monastery the retinue of the State Oracle of Tibet performed a special dance. In many of the colleges within Drepung Monastery, Achi Lhamo dance was performed on the last day of the sixth month and on the first day of the seventh month as a type of graduation ceremony for monks who had earned their Geshe degrees in philosophy and logic.

LHAMO GAR

Gar is the name of two different types of dance. One—as mentioned in the previous chapter—is a form of Cham that is not for public view. The other is a secular aristocratic dance that was performed in the courts of the Dalai Lama and other important monasteries within Tibet. Gar dances are performed on special occasions such as the first few days of the New Year *(Losar)* and the enthronement of a Dalai Lama. The Monlam Festival, while primarily a holy celebration, included an elaborate secular Gar performance, such as the *Tsongs Mchod Ser Bang,* "The Procession of the Offerings of the Assembly," created by Desi Sangye, the regent of the Fifth Dalai Lama, to memorialize the day of the death of the Great Fifth.

GARTOKPA— CEREMONIAL COURT DANCE

In olden times, an eighty-member Gar troupe called the *Gar-pa Kyi-do* was maintained by the palace. Young boys from good homes and in excellent health between the ages of seven and fourteen were recruited for the troupe and expected to serve for twelve years as Gar performers. A boy's service was considered as payment of a tax *(khral)* levied upon the family. In turn, his family was given tax exemptions on its land. Life for a young Gar dancer was severe, with practice in singing and dancing lasting from early morning until late at night. After almost two years he was considered trained and could go to school. However, he was kept under strict discipline and beaten if he misbehaved. When he grew up his reward could be a clerical post in a government office. Even after a member left the ensemble for adult life, he could be asked by the *gar pon* (leader) to participate in special performances.

Gar is different from most other dances in that there is no rapid foot stamping or spinning. Its movements are mostly hops and kicks without any sustained rhythm, causing it to appear oddly jerky. At the conclusion of the dance the performers shuffle out backward in single file and bend low in homage to their patrons. After a Gar performance, laypeople often dance in a circle, men on one side and women on the other.

Tibetan women dancing at Khangra, 1910–20. Photo by David MacDonald

⊡ The Dalai Lama Recalls Boyhood Shoton ⊡

PERFORMANCE IN ONE OF THE MONASTERIES OF
THE MOUNTAINS, TURN OF THE 20TH CENTURY

(These remarks are from an address about Achi Lhamo delivered at a special Shoton Festival on April 20, 1992, in Dharamsala, India.)

When I was young I enjoyed this festival because on that day I would get a day off from my regular study and also it was a spectacular event with a military parade. Shoton was, therefore, a happy event. The last Shoton festival I attended in Tibet was in 1958.

Generally speaking, in the past in Tibet not much recognition and importance was accorded to the opera artists. Opera or Lhamo was considered as any other common spectacle and it was not least considered as representing a nation's cultural heritage, way of thinking, lifestyles and social etiquettes. Excepting a few who may have had a genuine interest in Lhamo, on the whole, Lhamo artists themselves performed it partly as an obligation; it was as though certain groups and families had an obligation to perform Lhamo. It is for this reason that there was no serious motivation to improve and promote this artistic performance except to fulfill a given responsibility on occasions such as this.

Coming into exile, our most immediate concern was the preservation of our spiritual, cultural and Tibetan identity. We have, therefore, taken interest in and given attention to the Tibetan performing arts since 1959.

One thing is clear, that singing aria almost seems to be an inborn talent and unless you have efficient vocal cords from birth it is difficult to acquire it. Perhaps it is possible after a long and hard training. For instance, a number of Tibetan dances are performed by Chinese artists wearing Tibetan dress but so far I have never heard of a Chinese artist who could sing Tibetan arias just like a Tibetan. Likewise, it is also difficult for a Tibetan artist to perform a long bearded Chinese classical dance. Lhamo is, therefore, uniquely Tibetan because it is not possible for anybody else even to mimic it properly.

Several of the Opera singers today have good voices and efficient vocal cords. To sing arias, it is important to possess a good voice and flexible vocal cords too. I have never sung an opera song and I do not know how to sing it. Moreover, I am not allowed to sing. Nevertheless, I can differentiate between a good and a poor singer.[5]

A GROUP OF MASKED DANCERS READY FOR A
PERFORMANCE, TURN OF THE 20TH CENTURY

OPERA SEASONS

On the first day of the seventh Tibetan month, the four leading Lhamo troupes—known as the Gyangkhara, Chungpa, Shangpa, and Kyormol-ungpa—would journey to the Dalai Lama's summer home, the Jewel Park at the Norbulingka, for the opera season, known as Shoton. *Shoton* translates as "curd banquet," and yogurt was traditionally eaten each day of the celebration. The Shoton Festival originated at Drepung Monastery as a celebration of the end of the monks' annual summer retreat. The green pastures of that time of year ensured ample offerings of rich milk to the monasteries from which yogurt was made and distributed to everyone.

Beginning in medieval times, Shoton became more elaborate over the centuries, growing in popularity to become a national celebration of opera, still celebrated today by the Tibetan government-in-exile. It moved from Drepung to the Norbulingka Palace after it was built by the Eighth Dalai Lama in 1783. All of the performances took place outdoors under tents adorned with a statue of Thangtong Gyalpo, around which juniper branches and a bowl of barley flour were placed. The first day consisted of initiation dances performed by each troupe, lasting about twenty minutes each. The following days were showcases for the troupes, which presented operas that typically lasted up to eight hours. The Gyangkhara troupe was known for its ancient rough and serious style taken from Cham dancing and the Chungpa troupe had a high-pitched singing style and acrobatics. The Shangpa troupe from western Tibet used a lot of references from local folklore. The Kyormolungpa troupe from the Lhasa area was the newest as well as the most colorful and creative in its songs, choreography, and comic relief.

MONKS WITH LONG TRUMPETS IN TIBET AT THE TURN OF THE 20TH CENTURY

TIBETAN SACRED DANCE

At the end of an opera season, the best dancers from each troupe were given gifts by the Dalai Lama in the form of gold earrings. Then the troupes would go back to their provinces, often performing at different villages and monasteries along the way. All the troupes were rewarded with free ferry passes and grazing privileges for their livestock while they traveled, as well as being exempt from paying taxes, which were usually levied on the less fortunate in the form of grain quotas. They were also presented with sacks of grain, butter, and tea, along with some money to be divided among them at the end of their tour.

As the performances were given in lieu of tax, the government required the troupes to come to Lhasa by a certain date and give a specific number of performances at the Shoton Festival under the supervision of the *Tsechak Lekhung,* the treasury office of the central government. *Kyasel,* or lay monks, evaluated the quality of performances and appointed new actors and teachers, usually in a specific park just for that purpose called the Tsidevlingka. They published the programs and gave out the costumes and masks. They also doled out punishment when necessary if anyone did not do as he was told. Acting was restricted by the government in Lhasa to one month every year. After that, "not a drum was to be beaten nor a song to be sung" by any troupe.

LEOPARD DANCER IN BHUTAN. PHOTO BY CHÖGYAM TRUNGPA, 1968

OPPOSITE: DORJE
TROLLO

In addition to the four regional opera troupes, the government had its own official troupe of about forty performers, the Kyimolong. After Shoton, the Kyimolong troupe would be divided into groups of two to be sent to perform in different localities outside of the capital city. While waiting for their official papers, the performers and their families would buy silk, porcelain, jewelry, and other objects to sell along the way as they toured.

Another opera season took place during Losar, the New Year celebrations. Just after New Year's, each troupe would send out some of its actors after breakfast to dance in prominent civilians' houses, where they would make jokes or pretend to be beggars. Then the Gar-pa troupe of young dancers belonging specifically to the Dalai Lama would perform.

EPILOGUE

The question of where Tibetan dance has come from leads to the question of where it is going, a question this book can only raise, not answer. Tibetan dance—along with all Tibetan culture, philosophy, and religious practice— has been profoundly impacted by the Communist Chinese invasion and annexation of the Land of the Snows. Since that time the Chinese have deliberately and systematically attempted to wipe out the Tibetan people and their beliefs through vicious policies of forced sterilization of women, repopulation of the so-called Autonomous Region of Tibet by ethnic Han Chinese (thereby making Tibetans a minority in their own land), outlawing or severely restricting the teaching of Tibetan Buddhism, and refusing to allow Tibetan children to learn the Tibetan language in their own schools. A two-tiered economic system exists, with the best jobs and consumer goods going to the Chinese immigrants.

Hundreds of thousands of Tibetans have fled this persecution and now reside in India and around the world. Because of this tragic diaspora, the world has been bequeathed the ability to view the cultural gems of Tibet.

CHAM DEER DANCE
PERFORMED IN EXILE
(INDIA)

Tibetan painting, sculpture, and crafts are traded in both a free and black market and Tibetan Buddhist philosophy has seen a tremendous popular growth in the West. Now that Tibetans have made progress in establishing themselves in India and abroad, funds have been found to train monks and laypeople in dance and send them out to tour both within their own community and throughout the greater world.

THE TIBETAN INSTITUTE OF PERFORMING ARTS

WOMEN REHEARSING LHAMO AT TIPA

The initial goal of the Tibetan refugee community was just to survive each day, as many were relocated to inhospitable environments and had extremely limited means. Even so, the preservation of Tibetan culture was deemed so important

that the Tibetan Institute of Performing Arts (TIPA) was established in 1959 in Kalimpong, India, a well-known hill station on the road to Sikkim in the Himalayas. Then in 1960, it moved to Dharamsala along with the Dalai Lama. Fifteen or sixteen boys and girls were chosen from the Tibetan Children's Village to learn Achi Lhamo, for which they were paid a pittance—ten rupees a month. In 1962 the troupe performed for ten days at the Hindu Festival, where the chief minister of the Punjab was so impressed he gave them a five-hundred rupee gift. But the troupe still suffered from poor conditions for many years.

In 1975 TIPA had its first Western tour, performing the *Pema Woebar* opera about Padmasambhava's lotus flower birth. With a new director and an infusion of funds for teacher training from the Ford Foundation, the institute began to flourish. New operas were added and others revived. The school suffered a setback in 1984 when a fire destroyed most of its quarters and costumes, but—with tremendous sacrifice and tenacity—it persevered and today there are over sixty members. When the Dalai Lama was awarded the Nobel Peace Prize, TIPA performed *Gyalsa Bhelsa* at the Tibetan Children's Village School for the public and *Prince Norsang* for His Holiness.

Lobsang Samten's class, New York City

Members are divided into teachers, junior teachers, general performers, musicians, and trainees. New members apprentice for at least a year before becoming full members. Their studies include choreography, music, voice, and memorization of opera texts. As they grow in ability, they take on more important roles. Most plays are about two hours in length, though longer versions are done for special occasions. TIPA now conducts an annual Shoton Festival in Dharamsala, continues to tour throughout the world, and has recorded an album in Japan called "Drayang."

NEW FORMS

Now young Tibetans in India, and in Europe and North America, are exposed to Indian Bollywood musicals and Western pop and rap music. Growing up in exile, they are struggling with conflicts about their ethnic identity, attempting to assimilate into their host countries, and trying to figure out what inside of

NAWANG KECHOG,
GRAMMY AWARD–
NOMINATED TIBETAN
FLUTE PLAYER

them is truly Tibetan. Lay Tibetan musicians and performers are merging traditional forms with more modern ones, such as in the recordings of the fine
operatic voice of Tsering Wangmo—a classically trained Lhamo performer—
and of Dadon, who was forced to flee Tibet in 1992 because of her pro-Tibetan
tunes. The wildly popular Yungchen Lhamo appeals not only to young
Tibetans, but to people from around the world as well. There is also the etheric
music of Grammy-nominated Nawang Kechog and the recording of the nuns
of Nagi Gompa with Choying Drolma and the American Steve Tibbets. Chaksampa—a United States–based Lhamo group composed of performers originally trained at TIPA—also records and performs internationally.

STEVE GORN, MASTER
BANSURI FLUTE
PLAYER, AND NAWANG
KECHOG

CHAM TODAY

Several troupes of performing monks now tour the world, representing and raising funds to support their monasteries. They include monks from the Drepung Monastery, the Tashi Lumpo Monastery (founded by the First Dalai Lama in 1447), the Gaden Shartse monks, the Namgyal monks from the Dalai Lama's own monastery in Dharamsala, and the Gyuto tantric monks best known for their mesmerizing voices. The Drepung Loseling monks—featured in the Golden Globe–nominated soundtrack of *Seven Years in Tibet*—also performed with the composer Philip Glass in the live premier presentation of Glass's Academy Award–nominated score of Martin Scorsese's film *Kundun* and more Cham troupes will tour in the future.

The original purpose of Cham was to bring down blessings, banish evil forces, and spiritually empower the population within the context of their own culture. In Tibet before 1959, a Cham dance cycle could take up to a week to complete. In exile, because of the tastes of younger Tibetans, that time has been truncated. Even in Tibet, Cham performances have been affected, as shown by

MONKS LEAVING
AN INITIATION

the Tashilhunpo Monastery's recent shortening of what used to be two weeks' worth of performances down to three days. In Ladakh, Cham has been moved from its traditional performance time in the winter to the summer months to fit in with the demands of the tourist season, a phenomenon that further erodes its sacred nature. As Tibetan Cham troupes tour more often, the length of a performance is often severely cut to conform to Western sensibilities, available performance facilities, or even local labor union work hours.

Still, Cham continues to fulfill its sacred purpose even in modern times. When the Dalai Lama or other lamas perform a Kalachakra initiation—a twelve-day event that takes place in different locations throughout the world—one of the highlights occurs when monks enter the stage in brilliant brocade costumes and slowly circumambulate a raised dais called a *thekpu,* which will house a sand mandala. They must first perform the Dance of the Ground, or Sa-gar, to magnetize and then banish the local obstructing spirits by using strong steps and forceful kicks. The sight is so spectacular that even though there might be thousands of people attending, everyone falls silent. "They are dancing to make the land and the air fill with positive energy," was the spontaneous response of one Italian student.

Over the thirty-some years that I have been a Buddhist, an understanding of dance and how it is an outgrowth of the entire system of the tantras has woven in and out of my own practice and study. The kindness and infinite patience of my teachers have helped me to learn the true meaning and purpose of Cham, and the resources and assistance of the Tibetan Institute of the Performing Arts and the Tibetan Library of Works and Archives in Dharmasala have revealed the many facets of Achi Lhamo, enabling me to offer this book as an introduction. I hope it will encourage my readers to seek out performances with open minds and hearts and to be inspired and enlightened by the mysteries and wonders of Tibetan sacred dance.

NOTES

Part One

1. Keith Dowman, *Sky Dancer: The Secret Life and Songs of the Lady Yeshe Tsogyel* (London: Arkana, 1989), 99.

2. Rene de Nebesky-Wojkowitz, *Tibetan Religious Dances* (The Hague: Mouton, 1976).

3. Rene de Nebesky-Wojkowitz, *Tibetan Religious Dances,* 113.

4. Yeshe Tsogyel, *The Life and Liberation of Padmasambhava,* 2 vols., trans. Kenneth Douglas and Gwendolyn Bays (Berkeley: Dharma Publishing, l978), 384.

5. Glenn H. Mullin, *The Fourteen Dalai Lamas* (Santa Fe: Clear Light Publishers, 2001), 262.

6. W. N. Fergusson, *Adventure, Sport, and Travel on the Tibetan Steppes* (London: Constable and Co., 1911).

7. Author transcription from the Library of Tibetan Works and Archives, Dharamsala, India.

8. Keith Dowman, *Sky Dancer: The Secret Life and Songs of the Lady Yeshe Tsogyel,* 101.

9. Keith Dowman, *Sky Dancer: The Secret Life and Songs of the Lady Yeshe Tsogyel,* 91.

10. Dr. Alexander Fedotev, "Evolution of Tibetan Chams Tradition in Central Asia," *The Tibet Journal,* XI, no. 2, 50–55.

11. Rene de Nebesky-Wojkowitz, *Tibetan Religious Dances.*

12. Rene de Nebesky-Wojkowitz, *Tibetan Religious Dances,* 101.

13. Rene de Nebesky-Wojkowitz, *Tibetan Religious Dances.*

14. Rene de Nebesky-Wojkowitz, *Tibetan Religious Dances.*

15. The other great kings of the four directions are Phakyepu, Chenmigsang, and

Namthose. They are protectors of the Dharma. They are usually painted in thangkas or on the entrance walls of temples. They also danced in a Cham to commemorate the death of Desi Sangye Gyatso, the regent of the Fifth Dalai Lama.

16. Tibetan Government in Exile's Official Web Site, Nechung Page: http://www.tibet.com/Buddhism/nechung_hh.html

17. Rene de Nebesky-Wojkowitz, *Tibetan Religious Dances,* 243.

18. Captain Samuel Turner, *An Account of an Embassy to the Court of the Teshoo Lama in Tibet Containing a Narrative of a Journey Through Bootan, and Part of Tibet* (1800; reprint, New Delhi: Manjusri Publishing House, 1971), 307–08.

19. His Holiness the Dalai Lama, *Collected Statements, Interviews and Articles,* (Dharamsala: Department of Information and International Relations, 1982).

20. His Holiness the Dalai Lama, *Collected Statements, Interviews and Articles* (Dharamsala: Department of Information and International Relations, 1982).

Part Two

1. Tibetan Institute of Performing Arts Drama School Catalog (Dharamsala, 1990), 5.

2. Chaksampa Lhamo Dance Troupe, interview by author, 1991.

3. Evariste Régis Huc and Joseph Gabet, *Travels in Tartary, Thibet and China, 1844–1846,* edited by Paul Pelliot and translated by William Hazlitt, 2 vols. (1925; reprint, New Delhi: Asian Educational Series, 1988).

4. Hamilton Boner, *Diary of a Journey Across Tibet* (1894; reprint, Kathmandu: Ratna Pustak Bhandar, 1976), 166–67.

5. Dalai Lama, *Address* delivered at a special Shoton Festival on April 20, 1992, in Dharamsala, India, translated by Ngodup Tsering, former director of TIPA, and edited by Tenzin Dorjee and Merlin Willcox.

BIBLIOGRAPHY

An-Che, Li. "Rnin-Ma-Pa: The Early Forms of Lamanism." *Journal of the Royal Asiatic Society* (1948): 159–60.

———. "Bon: The Magico-Religious Belief of the Tibetan Speaking Peoples." *Southwestern Journal of Anthropology* 4, no. 1 (1948): 31–42.

Aris, Michael. "Sacred Dances of Bhutan." *Natural History Magazine* (March 1980).

Attisani, Antonio. "Tibetan Secular Theater." *PAJ—A Journal of Performance and Art* 63 (September 1999): 1–12.

Batchelor, Stephen. *The Tibet Guide.* London: Wisdom Publications, 1987.

———. *The Awakening of the West.* London: HarperCollins, Aquarian, 1994.

Bechert, Heinz, and Richard Gombrich. *The World of Buddhism.* New York and London: Facts on File Publications, 1984.

Beresford, Brian. "Hemis Festival in Ladakh." *Tibet Review* 2.

Bernbaum, Edwin. *The Way to Shambhala.* Los Angeles: Jeremy P. Tharcher, Inc., 1980.

Boner, Hamilton. *Diary of a Journey Across Tibet.* 1894. Reprint Kathmandu: Ratna Pustak Bhandar, 1976.

Chaksampa Lhamo Dance Troupe. Interview by author. 1991.

Conze, Edward. *Buddhist Scriptures.* London: Penguin Classics, 1959.

Corzort, Daniel. *Highest Yoga Tantra.* Ithaca: Snow Lion Publications, 1986.

Crossley-Holland, Peter. "The Ritual Music of Tibet." *Tibet Review* 1.

"Dagger Blessing: The Tibetan Purpa Cult: Reflections and Material." Book Review. *The Tibet Journal* 14, no. 2 (Summer 1989): 61–64.

Dalai Lama, His Holiness, *Collected Statements, Interviews and Articles.* Dharamsala: Department of Information and International Relations, 1982.

———. *Kindness, Clarity and Insight.* Translated and edited by Jeffrey Hopkins. Ithaca: Snow Lion Publications, 1984.

———. *The Dalai Lama at Harvard.* Translated and edited by Jeffrey Hopkins. Ithaca: Snow Lion Publications, 1988.

———. *Address* delivered at Shoton Festival, April 20, 1992, in Dharamsala, India, translated by Ngodup Tsering, former director of TIPA, and edited by Tenzin Dorjee and Merlin Willcox.

———, et al. *Tantra in Tibet.* Ithaca: Snow Lion Publications, 1977.

——. Tibetan Government in Exile's Official Web Site, Nechung Page: http://www.tibet.com/Buddhism/nechung_hh.html

David-Neel, Alexandra. "To Lhasa in Disguise." *Wide World Magazine,* vol. 61 (April–September 1928).

Denishaw Personal Collections of Photographs. New Yok City Public Library, Lincoln Center Dance Library (March 1926): 470–510.

Dorath, Rock Pierre. "Dance Evolution in Tibet." *Educational Dances* 6, no. 9 (March 1939).

Dorjee, Lobsang. "Lhamo: The Folk Opera of Tibet." *The Tibet Journal* 9, no. 2.

Dorje, Shakya. "Tashi Jong." *Orientations Magazine* (July 1975).

Dowman, Keith. *The Power-Places of Central Tibet: A Pilgrim's Guide.* London: Routledge and Kegan Paul, 1988.

——. *Sky Dancer: The Secret Life and Songs of the Lady Yeshe Tsogyel.* London: Arkana, 1989.

Encyclopedia of World Art. New York: McGraw Hill Book Company, 1960.

Evans-Wentz, W. Y. *Tibetan Yoga and Secret Doctrines.* London: Oxford University Press, 1958.

Fanti, Mario. *Mani Rimdu, Nepal, The Buddhist Dance Drama of Tengpoche.* New Delhi: The English Bookstore, 1976.

Fedotev, Dr. Alexander. "Evolution of Tibetan Chams Tradition in Central Asia." *The Tibet Journal,* 11, no. 2, 50–55.

Fergusson, W. N. *Adventure, Sport and Travel on the Tibetan Steppes.* London: Constable and Co., 1911.

——. *Land and People of Tibet and China in the Early 20th Century.* Delhi: Sharda Prakashan, 1989.

Foster, Barbara, and Michael Foster. *Forbidden Journey: The Life of Alexandra David-Neel.* San Francisco: Harper & Row, 1987.

Fromaget, Alain. "Lhamo." *Chö Yang: The Voice of Tibetan Religion and Culture,* Year of Tibet Edition (1991).

Frye, Stanley, translator. "Who Was the Founder of the Bon Religion?" *Tibet Review* 1.

Getty, Alice. *The Gods of Northern Buddhism*. 1914. Reprint, New York: Dover Publications, 1988.

Govinda, Li Gotami. *Tibet in Pictures: A Journey to the Past,* vol. 1. Central Tibet, Dharma Publishing, 1979.

Hamel, Peter Michael. *Through Music to the Self.* England: Element Books, 1976.

Helffer, Mireille. *Mchod-rol: Les instruments de la musique tibétan.* Paris: CNRS Éditions, Éditions de la Maisons des Sciences de l'Homme, n.d.

Heller, Amy. "Historic and Iconographic Aspects of the Protective Deities Srung-ma Dmar-nag."

Hitchcock, John T. "Stones, Bones & Skin. Ritual & Shamanic Art, Nepali Shaman's Performance." *Arts Canada* (December '73/January '74).

Huc, Evariste Régis. *Recollections of a Journey through Tartary, Thibet, and China*, vol. 1. New York: Appleton, 1852.

——, and Joseph Gabet. *Travels in Tartary, Thibet and China, 1844–1846.* Edited by Paul Pelliot and translated by William Hazlitt. 2 vols. 1925. Reprint, New Delhi: Asian Educational Series, 1988.

Jackson, Janice, and David Jackson. *Tibetan Thangka Painting: Methods and Materials.* Ithaca: Snow Lion Publications, 1984.

Jaffrey, Madhur. "Buddhist Dance Spectacular in a Medieval Kingdom." *Asia Magazine* (March/April 1980).

Jerstad, Luther G. *Mani Rimdu Sherpa Dance and Drama.* Seattle: University of Washington Press, 1969.

Journal of the American Oriental Society, Baltimore. 69, #2 (April–June, 1949): 51–59.

Kawaguchi, Ekai. *Three Years in Tibet.* 1909. Reprint, Kathmandu: Ratna Pustak Bhandar, 1979.

Knapp, Dr. Bettina C. "Shamanism and Trance Dance." *Arabesque* 6, no. 3 (September/October 1980).

Kohn, Richard Jay. *Mani Rimdu: Text and Tradition in a Tibetan Ritual.* Ph.D. diss., University of Wisconsin, 1988.

Kvaerne, Per. *A Norwegian Traveller in Tibet.* New Delhi: Manjusri Publishing, 1973.

LaMein Collection, Tibet. "4 Devil Dances at the Mt. Everest Hotel." New York City Public Library, Lincoln Center Dance Library (ca. 1927).

Landor, A. H. S. *Tibet, The Forbidden Land.* 1899. Reprint, Delhi: Gian Publications, 1980.

Lerner, Lin. "Two Tibetan Ritual Dances: A Comparative Study." *Tibet Review* 3.

Lhalungpa, Lobsang P. "Tibetan Music: Secular and Sacred." *The Tibet Society Newsletter* 2 (1968): 8–17.

Lopon Tenzin Namdak Rinpoche, Bön Master. Private interview by author, New York City, 1991.

Lucas, Heinz. *Lamaistische Maske.* Kassel: Erich-Röth-Verlag, 1962.

Marini, Fosco. *Secret Tibet.* New York: Viking Press, 1952.

Marshall, Sir John. *The Buddhist Art of Gandhara.* New Delhi: Oriental Books Reprint Corp., 1980.

Migot, Andre. *Tibetan Marchers.* New York: E. P. Dutton and Co., 1955.

Mullin, Glenn H. *The Fourteen Dalai Lamas.* Santa Fe: Clear Light Publishers, 2001.

Nebesky-Wojkowitz, Rene de. *Tibetan Religious Dances.* The Hague: Mouton, 1976.

Newark Museum Catalogue of Tibetan Collection, vol. II, *Sculpture and Painting.* Newark, N.J.: The Newark Museum, 1986.

Norbu, Jamyang. *Zlos-Gar.* Dharamsala: Library of Tibetan Works and Archives, 1986.

Norbu, Namkhai. *The Song of the Vajra.* Conway, Mass.: Dzogchen Community of America, 1992.

Patterson, George N. *Journey with Loshay.* New York: W. W. Norton and Co., 1954.

Rawson, Philip. *The Art of Tantra.* London: Thames and Hudson, 1973.

——. *The Body in Tantra.* In *The Body as a Medium of Expression.* Edited by J. Benthall and T. Polhemus. London: Allen Lane, 1975.

Rhie, Marilyn M., and Robert Thurman. *Wisdom and Compassion: The Sacred Art of Tibet.* New York: Harry Abrams, 1991.

Rigzin, Tsepak. *Festivals of Tibet.* Dharamsala: Library of Tibetan Works and Archives, 1993.

Rinpoche, Kalu. *The Dharma That Illuminates All Beings Impartially Like the Light of the Sun and Moon.* New York: State University Press of New York, 1977.

——. *Teachings on Artist's Role in the Dharma.* Tape, 1982.

Rinpoche, Tulku Thondup. *Hidden Teachings of Tibet: An Explanation of the Terma Tradition of the Nyingma School of Buddhism.* London: Wisdom Publications, 1986.

Ritual Dance Master, Mani Rimdu Festival. Taped interview by author during Kalachakra Initiation, New York City, 1991.

Rock, Joseph F. "Life Among the Lamas of Choni." *National Geographic Magazine* 54 (November 1928): 569–614.

——. "With the Devil Dancers of China and Tibet." *National Geographic Magazine* 60 (July 1931): 18–59.

——. "Demon Possessed Tibetans & Their Incredible Feats." *National Geographic Magazine* 68 (October 1935): 479–86.

Samten, Lobsang, Ritual Dance Master, Namygal Monastery. Interview by author. 1991.

Samuel, Geoffrey. "The Vajrayana in the Context of Himalayan Folk Religion."

Schrempf, Mona. "From 'Devil Dance' to 'World Healing': some representations, perceptions and innovations of contemporary Tibetan ritual dances." In *Tibetan Culture in the Diaspora.* Edited by F. J. Korom. Vienna: Verlag der Österreichischen Akademie der Wissenschaften, 1997. 91–102.

Shaw, Brian. "Bhutan, Land of the Dragon People." *7th Festival of Asian Art.* The Urban Council, 1982.

Shawn, Ted. "Demon Dances of Tibet." *The Dance* (September 1926).

Singh, N. "The Collective Vajrakilaya Retreat." *The Tibet Journal* 14, no. 2 (Summer 1989): 49–55.

Snellgrove, David. *Indo-Tibetan Buddhism,* vol. 1. Boston: Shambhala Publications, 1987.

——, and Hugh Richardson. *A Cultural History of Tibet.* Boston: Shambhala Publishing, 1986.

"A Spectrum of World Dance Tradition, Transition and Innovation." *Dance Research Annual: Selected Papers from the 1982/83 CORD Conferences* 16 (1987).

Sperling, Elliot. "Notes on References to Bri-Gung-pa—Mongol Contact in the Late Sixteenth and Early Seventeenth Centuries."

Tibet: The Sacred Realm, Photographs, 1880–1950. New York: Aperture, 1983.

"Tibetan Devil Dances." *The Dancing Times* (July 1935): 371.

Tibetan Institute of Performing Arts Drama School Catalog, Dharamsala, 1990.

Todd, B. K. "Bhutan, Land of the Thunder Dragon." *National Geographic Magazine* 102 (1952): 713, 754.

Trungpa, Chögyam. *Born in Tibet.* New York: Penguin Books, 1966.

——. *Crazy Wisdom.* Boston: Shambhala Publications, 1991.

——. *Orderly Chaos: The Mandala Principle.* Boston: Shambhala Publications, 1991.

Tsogyal, Yeshe. *The Life and Liberation of Padmasambhava.* 2 vols. Translated by Kenneth Douglas and Gwendolyn Bays. Berkeley: Dharma Publishing, 1978.

Tucci, Giuseppe. *The Temples of Western Tibet and Their Artistic Symbolism.* New Delhi: Aditya Prakashaw, 1935.

Tulru, Mynak R. "The Sacred Dance Drama of Bhutan." National Museum of Bhutan.

Turner, Captain Samuel. *An Account of An Embassy to the Court of the Teshoo Lama in Tibet Containing a Narrative of a Journey Through Bootan, and Part of Tibet.* 1800. Reprint, New Delhi: Manjusri Publishing House, 1971.

Ulmer, Spring. "An Endangered Art: Traditional Tibetan Music, Dance and Drama."

Wang, Ya. *Tales From Tibet Opera.* Beijing: New World Press, 1986.

Warder, A. K. *Indian Buddhism.* New Delhi: Motilal Banarsidas, 1970.

Whitfield, Roderick, and Ann Farrer. *Caves of the Thousand Buddhas.* London: British Museum Publications, 1990.

Williams, Joanna Gottfried. *The Art of Gupta India.* Princeton: Princeton University Press, 1980.

INDEX

Italic pages numbers indicate illustrations.